A Preference for the Poor

Latin American Liberation Theology from a Protestant Perspective

Manfred K. Bahmann

University Press of America,® Inc.
Lanham · Boulder · New York · Toronto · Oxford

BT
88.57
.B3213
2005

Copyright © 2005 by
University Press of America,® Inc.
4501 Forbes Boulevard
Suite 200
Lanham, Maryland 20706
UPA Acquisitions Department (301) 459-3366

PO Box 317
Oxford
OX2 9RU, UK

All rights reserved
Printed in the United States of America
British Library Cataloging in Publication Information Available

Library of Congress Control Number: 2004113393
ISBN 0-7618-3053-7 (paperback : alk. ppr.)

⊖™ The paper used in this publication meets the minimum
requirements of American National Standard for Information
Sciences—Permanence of Paper for Printed Library Materials,
ANSI Z39.48—1984

TABLE OF CONTENTS

Preface		v
I	Back to Where It All Started	1
II	Bogotá 1968—Papal Visit and Its Consequences	5
III	Medellín 1968—Now the Bishops Speak	9
IV	A Call to Repentance	13
V	Latin America Finds a Voice	19

    1. J.L. Segundo: The Principle of Suspicion 19
    2. J.P. Miranda: The Radical Love of the Bible 20
    3. L. Boff: A Voice for the Voiceless 22
    4. J. Sobrino: In the Footsteps of Jesus 25
    5. E. Dussel: The Conqueror and the Conquered 26
    6. Summary 29

VI	The Revolution That Never Came	33
VII	Roma Locuta Est	37
VIII	A Preferential Option for the Poor	43
IX	What Is Left?	51
X	Why Should We Care?	59
XI	The Excluded	65
XII	Faith That Moves Mountains	73

    1. Origin and Growth of the Pentecostals 73
    2. Seized by an Incomprehensible Force 75
    3. The Word Creating Miracles 78
    4. Work of the Spirit? 80

XIII	Responsibility—A Protestant Perspective	83

    1. Living in Exile 83
    2. The Two Realms 87
    3. The Sore Point 89
    4. The Priesthood of All Believers 91
    5. The Ongoing Work of Creation 94

Bibliography	97
Index	101
Author Biographical Sketch	103

PREFACE

This small volume has been a long time in coming. Ever since I was an ecumenical observer at the 1968 Conference of the Latin American Bishops in Medellín, Colombia, I have strongly supported the radical new vision for the church and the continent that arose there, called Latin American Liberation Theology. As a Lutheran theologian and a professor for church history in Argentina for five years, I did not always find myself in complete agreement with the points made by its advocates. But I have closely followed the unfolding and flourishing of this theological project over the decades, and always defended its basic thrust and direction.

Yet things have become very quiet in this corner of theological activity in recent years. For some time there was hardly a peep, let alone a noteworthy work, on the current state of Latin American Liberation Theology. This quiescence made me very uneasy. Thus, when a grant from the Samuel Trexler Fellowship of the Metropolitan New York Synod of the Evangelical Lutheran Church in America became available, along with continuing education funds from National Lutheran Campus Ministry, I seized the opportunity to return to Buenos Aires in the summer of 1998. I wanted to find some answers.

The results of my investigation, along with some historical and theological analyses of Latin American Liberation Theology, are presented here. Admittedly quite a number of people have issued a death certificate for this theological undertaking. But I do not share that judgment. The pressing human problems out of which a distinctive liberation theology arose in Latin America remain unsolved. The crying needs this Roman Catholic initiative sought to articulate have not been answered. The call to reform and repentance issued by these liberationists is as valid today as it was in 1968. Until this call is answered, Latin American Liberation Theology cannot be declared dead. Meanwhile, this author is convinced that it can benefit from a Protestant voice.

The movement had something close to a near-death experience as church and society in Latin America took a more conservative direction in the 1970's, followed by the worldwide collapse of Marxist socialism in 1989. Clearly liberation theology on the subcontinent will not return to health unless it finds a new, solidly theological foundation. I agree with Robin Nagle, who in a study of the situation in Brazil came to the following sad conclusion:

> Liberation theology . . . is found today more in the remnants of what it tried to become than in an active, vibrant practice of what it promised. Advocates often professed a Catholicism that better reflected the aspirations of those bringing the liberation message than the needs of the people to whom the message was directed.

> The movement's biggest weaknesses were its inability to recognize the role of crucial historic, political, and economic forces that shaped the choices of 'the poor', those meant to be 'liberated' by this new Catholicism, and its inability to appreciate that 'the poor' cannot be met as an undifferentiated collection of people with the same world view, needs, and desires (Nagle, *Claiming the Virgin*, p. 24).

Robin Nagle has presented an anthropological inquiry into this subject. Others, most importantly Jean-Pierre Bastian and Antonio O. Donini, have engaged in sociological research. My focus is historical and theological. The church historian in me wants to know: What has become of Latin American Liberation Theology? What happened? How did we get from there to here? The theologian in me asks: What is its meaning, if any, today? What does it signify for the Christian faith?

After an explanation of my personal involvement, I give an eyewitness account of Pope Paul VI's 1968 visit to Bogotá and a description of the subsequent proceedings at the CELAM Bishops' Conference in Medellín. I discuss the call to repentance issued by Gustavo Gutiérrez in *A Theology of Liberation* (original Spanish version published in 1971). I present the contributions of five prominent Latin American liberation theologians, followed by a chapter on the impact of the Latin American military dictatorships in the second half of the 1970's. After an analysis of the new direction given to Roman Catholic theology by Pope Paul VI in 1975, I show how these papal guidelines were taken up in the 1979 CELAM Bishops' Conference in Puebla, Mexico. I describe a roundtable discussion during my visit in July 1998 with some of the faculty at I.S.E.D.E.T. (Instituto Superior Evangélico de Estudios Teológicos), the Protestant union seminary in Buenos Aires, on the state of Latin American Liberation Theology since the fall of the Berlin Wall. After reflecting on the present situation in Latin America, especially recent shifts in its religious map, I discuss the relationship of Roman Catholicism to this theology in recent years and give an account of the rapidly growing Pentecostal presence across the continent. Finally I offer a Protestant perspective that could provide new hope and direction to Latin American liberation.

The author acknowledges with thanks the following permissions to include extended copyrighted selections: John L. Kater, Jr., "Whatever Happened to Liberation Theology?" in *Anglican Theological Review* 83/4 (fall 2001), used in chapter 11; William B. Eerdmans Publishing Company, Grand Rapids, MI, for Richard Shaull and Waldo Cesar, *Pentecostalism and the Future of the Christian Churches* (2000), quoted throughout chapter 12; and Orbis Books, Maryknoll, NY for Gustavo Gutiérrez, *A Theology of Liberation*, 15th anniversary edition (1988), which as the seminal source on Latin American Liberation Theology is cited throughout this work.

A stylistic note is necessary. The term "liberation theology" has come to be used in various contexts over the decades. Where Liberation Theology is capitalized in this text, it refers specifically to the Latin American version.

I am much indebted to a number of my former students for their gracious hospitality during my stay in Buenos Aires. Dr. Arturo Blatezky was a generous host and an excellent guide; he brought me into contact with church groups still practising this theology today in Argentina. Pastors Bruno Knoblauch, Rodolfo Reinich, Juan Pedro Schaad, and Federico Schaefer gave freely of their time and provided helpful advice.

I thank my former colleagues at I.S.E.D.E.T., especially Dr. José Míguez Bonino and Dr. Ricardo Pietrantonio, for some valuable insights. Several other members of the faculty—Drs. Nancy Bedford, Willy Hansen, and Pablo Andiñach—also helped to clarify the picture.

Father Rafael Braun, former editor of *Criterio* and Director of the Centro de Espiritualidad Santa María in Palermo, Buenos Aires, guided me through some important documents of Roman Catholic teaching. I also received helpful suggestions on relevant literature from my colleagues in Lutheran Campus Ministry Drs. John Hougen and Luther Kriefall. And my deep gratitude goes to my wife Marianne for her constant encouragement and careful stylistic review of this manuscript.

Manfred K. Bahmann

Pocono Lake, Pennsylvania
July 2004

I
BACK TO WHERE IT ALL STARTED

"From the very beginning, Liberation Theology has been intellectually bankrupt."
Father Rafael Braun in a personal conversation with the author in Buenos Aires on July 22, 1998.

"What will remain of the 'theology of liberation' in a few short years? The question may seem to be pessimistic in tone, suggesting that liberation theology was a superficial thing or a passing fad. That is certainly not the case. My question should be approached in a positive and hopeful spirit." (Juan Luis Segundo, *The Liberation of Theology*, p. 3)

This is the question Juan Luis Segundo poses at the beginning of his book on the liberation of theology. What will remain? It is the same question with which he opened his lectures on the subject at Harvard University in 1974. Today we raise the question again, but not in a future sense of what will remain. Today we ask in a past sense: What if anything is left of Liberation Theology?

When Segundo gave his lectures at Harvard and then published them in 1975 as *Liberación de la Teología* (the English translation appeared in 1976), he very much wanted this new theology to be fully accepted in the universities and academic centers of the world. From its very beginning it was a "theology rising out of the urgent problems of real life" as he put it (p. 4). It was in every sense a theology firmly rooted in the biblical interpretation and in the dogmatic tradition, feeling a responsibility "toward both the problems of real life and the canons of worldwide theology" (p. 5). Yet Segundo left no doubt that Latin American Liberation Theology moved forward "without the erudite exploration and attention to detail which is evident when a new line of theological thought is introduced into present-day European or North American theology. In affirming certain essential points, moreover, it left aside other points which may have been important in their consequences" (ibid.).

Segundo considered the normal theology taught in seminaries and universities too academic, a theology just of books. Thus, he claimed, while Latin American Liberation Theology evoked an interest among the non-initiated it also stirred up "a certain amount of academic disdain from the great centers of theological thought around the world" (ibid.). He was right. And the struggle has continued. This same tension between interest and disdain still exists today.

During a month-long visit of inquiry to Argentina, I received conflicting responses when I asked what remains of this theological project. Answers ranged from the dismissive declaration that "Liberation Theology is dead" to a contemptuous comment that "It never amounted to anything, it was always intellectually bankrupt," and on to the equally firm assurance that "Oh, no, it is still very much alive and energizing the life of the church and our ministry."

Liberation Theology is still a fascinating phenomenon. While it tends to divide people and polarize them on issues that concern all of us, it also helps attentive observers to sharpen their senses as they struggle to understand our present world and the events that shape it. Latin American Liberation Theology was born in 1968. The ground had been prepared by the emergence of the *comunidades de base*, grass roots communities of Christian lay people that indicated something new was in the air. These expressions of a new popular spiritual stirring had been rapidly spreading in several Latin American countries, especially Brazil. As with pregnancy, new life was pushing to be born. At the conference of the Latin American Bishops in Medellín in August of that year, this theology would enter the world and emit its first piercing cries.

The new birth was duly registered in North America and Europe. But it did not command a lot of attention at first. Other, more important issues occupied the theological agenda. That changed a few years later when several brilliant, eye-catching analyses by Latin American theologians began to appear on the scene. First to capture attention, as we noted in the preface, was Gustavo Gutiérrez in 1971 with his controversial *A Theology of Liberation*. Others soon followed: Hugo Assmann, Rubem Alves, Leonardo Boff, Julio de Santa Ana, Enrique Dussel, José Míguez Bonino, José Miranda, Jon Sobrino, Juan Luis Segundo, Severino Croatto, to name the most prominent early contributors. Soon the flood of seminal thought by Latin American Liberation Theologians could no longer be overlooked by the world's academic and theological centers.

But over the next thirty years the flood gradually slowed to a trickle. During the 1990's not one significant work on Liberation Theology appeared. What happened? Was Segundo wrong with his strong declaration about the bright future of the new movement? Had this theology turned out to be just "a superficial and ephemeral fad" after all?

On an investigative trip in July 1998 to I.S.E.D.E.T. (Instituto Superior Evangélico de Estudios Teológicos), the Protestant seminary in Buenos Aires where the author had taught church history thirty years earlier, he found a number of significant changes in the theological climate. In 1968 there existed a consensus among the emerging Latin American liberationists that their countries were ripe for radical revolution, and it would be socialist in nature. When during the 1970's most of Latin American was ruled by military dictatorships or juntas with strong ties to entrenched capitalist oligarchies, the only answer theologians saw was a revolution shaped by Marxism.

But by the time of my visit in 1998, much had happened. The generals were out of power in Latin America. Most countries lived under one form or another of democracy. Socialism had collapsed after the Berlin Wall came down in 1989 and the Communist empire fell with a great crash as well. Karl Marx has been declared dead. His theories of class warfare and a takeover of the means of production by the proletariat will not be revived for a long time, if ever. This development had a profound impact upon liberation movements in Latin America and effectively silenced their theologians.

Yet we must still ask: What remains? Does Latin American Liberation Theology have anything meaningful to say to us anymore? Can it still provide any sort of direction for the future? And even more important, what was the root of its pulsing vitality?

These and other questions occupied my mind in Buenos Aires. As I sought to find answers in conversations and forums, I discovered that much of this theology's history and development has been forgotten, shoved aside, or misunderstood. As one who was present at its inception in Medellín and has followed its course from his Lutheran perch for decades, the author feels a personal responsibility to provide the following account as a historical and theological record, an eyewitness framework within which others who did not experience it first-hand may legitimately discuss and reflect.

II
BOGOTÁ 1968—A PAPAL VISIT AND ITS CONSEQUENCES

"Liberation Theology comes out of a concrete reality. Together with its context its perspectives have shifted in the last thirty years." Pablo Andiñach, Professor for Old Testament, in a panel discussion at I.S.E.D.E.T. on July 16, 1998.

Latin American Liberation Theology is contextual theology. It is not an academic exercise. It is born out of struggle. As Juan Luis Segundo put it, the theology arose "out of the urgent problems of real life" (Segundo, The Liberation of Theology, p. 4). The same must be said about the circumstances and the event through which it was born.

The Second General Conference of Latin American Bishops held at Medellín in 1968 was also embedded in a specific historical context. The assembly of the bishops was the result of two distinct movements. As we have observed, it was preceded by the spread of grass-root lay communities which had strongly influenced the thinking of these church leaders. But the assembly was also an element of the sweeping reforms resulting from the Second Vatican Council in Rome from 1963 to 1965 which now were changing the Roman Catholic Church all over the world.

When Vatican II concluded in December of 1965, it charged all the Roman Catholic bishops to apply the new concepts which had emerged in Rome to the life of the church in their respective countries. The Catholic Bishops in Latin America were assigned a clear task to accomplish locally what the Vatican Council had done for the universal church throughout the world. They were to carry out the program of aggiornamento in their region. Just as Pope John XXIII "opened the windows of the church to let in the fresh wind of the world," as he once said, Latin America's church leaders must now bring the churches under their wing up to date. They must allow the fresh, sometimes sharp wind of the world to blow through their venerable temples.

In spite of economic hardships, 1968 was a time of great hope and optimism. Revolutionary change was shaking foundations in many parts of the world. In China the infamous Red Guards were busy waging a cultural revolution. In Europe and North America students were demonstrating against the Vietnam War and demanding radical reforms in both universities and societies. At the same time, man had reached out to the moon and made the first voyage from earth to this faraway planet. Underlying all this was the conviction that things could be changed for the better. Reform was not only possible, it was the mandate of the hour.

Such was the mood that inspired the assembly of the bishops in Medellín. In keeping with the general thrust of Vatican II they gave their 1968 conference the title "The Church in the Present-Day Transformation of Latin America in the Light of the Council." With this title they indicated an openness to the changes and transformations that were going on outside church walls.

Their hopefulness was underscored by a powerful and unique event. For the first time in history the Roman Pontiff was visiting Latin America, the most Catholic of continents. Pope Paul VI had come to Colombia take part in a Eucharistic Congress in Bogotá, after which he would open the bishops' conference in the cathedral on August 24.

I had the good fortune to be present on both of these occasions, as the official representative of the Lutheran World Federation. Afterwards I would participate in the bishops' conference in Medellín as an ecumenical observer and honored guest. Two days earlier I had found myself in a vast field outside of Bogotá, in the midst of a huge throng awaiting the arrival of the Pope. The Pontiff was to receive the representatives of different Latin American ethnic groups, and a boisterous, joyful mood permeated the enormous crowd.

As a Lutheran pastor in a black suit and white clergyman's collar I was indistinguishable from any Roman Catholic priest in the throng. I struck up a conversation with one of them standing next to me. We had a friendly exchange until suddenly my new-found clergy friend noticed the wedding band on my left hand. Deeply concerned, he looked up and asked me: "My God, what is that?" Without revealing my Lutheran identity, I answered: "Soy casado! I am married!" His look of worry changed to horror— had it really come to this? Had they removed the requirement of celibacy? In the wake of Vatican II many had wondered whether the end of obligatory celibacy was at hand. My friend was greatly relieved when I revealed to him my Lutheran identity.

A few minutes later a helicopter carrying the Pope appeared above our heads. A tumultuous joy broke out in the crowd. I, too, the Lutheran heretic, unable to resist, happily waved a white handkerchief and shouted "Viva el Papa! Viva el Papa!"

During the days that followed, our ecumenical relations were cordial. But many unanswered questions hung in the air. We were all very much aware of how fragile the bond was that held us together. As I sat in the spacious choir area before the altar in the cathedral of Bogotá for the solemn opening of the bishops' conference, Paul VI was only a few feet away from me as he delivered his inaugural address. After the first few sentences we suddenly could not hear his words, we could only follow the movement of his lips. The microphone was on the blink. I shook my head wryly and thought: "My Latin American friends knock themselves out when the pope comes to visit for the first time, yet the mike doesn't work!"

I wondered what to do. All around me, splendidly robed prelates cardinals, archbishops, bishops sat impassively, heavy pectoral crosses resting on their massive chests. Then my eyes were drawn to the large crucifix above the altar. As I meditated on this cross, I heard the words of Martin Luther admonishing me: "Begin with the wounds of Christ! God comes to us not in his glory but in his humanity." Yes, I agreed. But then the thought took hold: "If you truly accept the simple humanity of your God, then do what human decency requires of you in this situation. Get up, take the few steps to the pope and tell the elderly gentleman from Italy that the mike is on the fritz!" Of course I did not do it. Courage failed me. I consoled myself with the thought that I was just a guest, not a full member of this household.

Then I noticed the worn, lined face of a prelate sitting across the aisle. He was wearing a simple alb and a wooden cross. Finding some comfort in the weathered features, I realized that this man was Dom Hélder Cámara, the renowned Archbishop of Olinda and Recife in northeastern Brazil. Meanwhile, one of the bishops had gone forward and interrupted the Holy Father. While we waited for the public address system to be repaired, we all sang a "Te Deum" until the pope could continue with his discourse.

The next day was a Sunday. I settled in to read the full text of the pope's address. As I did so, I thought about my impression of Pope Paul VI as a human being. He seemed so different from the popular, down-to-earth John XXIII. Paul VI was more of an aristocrat. Yet he seemed to be a spiritual man who thought deeply about many issues. But as I read and pondered the text more closely, I thought about its implications and my heart sank.

Several weeks earlier Paul VI had published the encyclica "Humanae Vitae" prohibiting any form of artifical birth control. There was no doubt as to whom this missive was directed. It delivered a clear, forceful message to the Christians in Latin America, a continent that was literally exploding with population growth. But here was an unambiguous No to the birth control pill. I had studied "Humanae Vitae" carefully on the flight to Bogotá and had become concerned already then. But now the pope's sermon of Saturday, August 24, 1968 filled me with a deepening worry.

In his address the pope tried to set the direction for the bishops' conference which was to follow during the next two weeks. He had three main points: 1) The Catholic Church should participate boldly in the social changes occurring in Latin America, seeking to "raise up the poor and all who live in conditions of human and social inferiority." 2) In doing so, the church should steer clear of "atheistic Marxism, systematic revolt, and of blood and anarchy." 3) He declared once again an intransigent and absolute prohibition of any artificial birth and population control. (The Church in the Present-Day Transfomation of Latin America in the Light of the Council, I Position Papers [hereafter abbreviated as Medellín I], p. 41f.)

I was dismayed and perplexed. I had lived for four years in Latin America, long enough to know that any two of the pope's three points made sense. But a combination of all three could not possibly work. One might be able to improve the lot of the poor in Latin America without bloodshed and anarchy, but a way must be found to control the raging population explosion. On the other hand, one could promote the well-being of the poor without artifical birth control, but this would invite violence and bloodshed. Trying to put all three demands together was completely unrealistic, like having your cake and eating it too.

That Sunday, as I thought about his sermon of the day before, Paul VI had already returned to Rome. That afternoon I was taken with the rest of the Latin American church leaders to the modern and comfortable seminary in Medellín. All the way, I turned over in my mind the question: How will these bishops respond to the direction set forth by the Holy Father? Will they swallow all three of his points? If not, what combination can they pursue?

I also wondered: How widely could the Latin American church leaders open the windows of their cathedrals? How much sharp wind from an often hostile world would they allow to blow through their venerable edifices? The next two weeks could well determine the future course of the church. I resolved to take copious notes.

III
MEDELLÍN 1968—NOW THE BISHOPS SPEAK

"Some of the impulses given by Liberation Theology have become stronger in the last years. This is true for example with the Bible study movement. The Bible is very much studied in the grass roots communities today." Pablo Andiñach, Professor of Old Testament, in a panel discussion at I.S.E.D.E.T. on July 16, 1998.

As the Bishops' Conference took up its proper business in Medellín on Monday, I was in for a tremendous surprise. I was introduced to a way of interpreting church documents that was completely new to me.

Although the bishops constantly quoted the pope, as I listened to them my Protestant mind told me that their use of his words did not reflect his exact meaning. In other words, they were massaging the pope's message. After a polite reference to him they would take off in another direction more to their liking, reaching conclusions not at all implied in the papal pronouncement. In the flash of a few short days I received a valuable education in how the Roman Catholic Church functions from the inside. At Medellín, each discrepancy between the pope's actual words and their subsequent interpretation by the assembled prelates opened a free space for the Holy Spirit to move and work. As I watched this process unfold, it occurred to me that by slavishly clinging to a written text we Protestants often tend to fill up such free spaces prematurely.

An indomitable spirit was at work in Medellín, a spirit every bit as joyfully infectious as the one I had experienced while waiting for the pope in the field outside Bogotá a few days earlier. I caught my breath as Avelar Brandao Vilela, the Archbishop of Teresina in Brazil and one of the conference's co-presidents, called for a new outpouring of the Holy Spirit upon Latin America. He demanded with great passion that the conference "become a new Pentecost" (Medellín I, p. 75). His call was seconded by the Argentine Bishop Eduardo Pironio, who later became a cardinal and then general secretary of the Episcopal Council. Pironio boldly asserted that they had come together "in the communion of the Spirit that assures and manifests the saving event of a new Pentecost for Latin America" (ibid., p. 111f). For a moment I felt as though I was not at a conference of staid Catholic bishops but in the communion of Pentecostal preachers!

Medellín was contextual theology. Its message came—to use Juan Juis Segundo's phrase once again—"rising out of the urgent problems of real life" (Segundo, *The Liberation of Theology*, p. 4) After opening speeches by several dignitaries, the conference was locked for a week in the grip of a clear-eyed presentation of the harsh realities that dominate life in Latin America. Some of the older, more formidable prelates fumed that they were being held captive by a corps of "experts." "What is all this nonsense?" they protested. "I have lived all my life in Latin America!" The "experts" they referred to were younger Jesuit and Franciscan theologians, who with some social scientists were in charge of the program during the first week. Using slides and statistical reports, these "experts" presented irrefutable evidence of the appalling living conditions in Latin America. Their presentation eradicated any doubt about the abject poverty of the masses, the widespread illiteracy and unemployment, the lack of decent housing and basic medical care, the flight of millions from the countryside to the burgeoning slums ringing every metropolitan area, and many other ills.

It was not until the second week that the majority of prelates were allowed to speak their mind. The conference participants were divided into working groups dealing with the themes of Peace, Justice, Family and Demography, and Education and Youth. I chose to be part of the commission on Justice. As an ecumenical guest I had no vote in the assembly, but in every other way I was treated as an equal, and I was chosen to be the secretary of our commission. During the days that followed I furiously took notes of our deliberations and worked very hard to compose a faithful set of minutes. Part of my effort even made its way into the final document—ecumenical cooperation in the best sense.

It has been said that the Medellín conference did not produce one single, coherent document but ended up—so the charge goes—with an array of committee reports that hang together only loosely. The importance of this criticism depends upon one's point of view. An attentive and sympathetic observer will see that indeed, Medellín does speak with one voice. It is a matter of having the right spirit.

On the issue of justice, for example, the bishops declare that "the misery that besets large masses ... in all of our countries ... as a collective fact expresses itself as injustice which cries to the heavens." They recognize the "almost universal frustration of legitimate aspirations which creates the climate of collective anguish in which we are already living" (*The Church in the Present-Day Transformation of Latin America in the Light of the Council*, Vol. II Conclusions [hereafter abbreviated as Medellín II], on Justice, no. 1). They are firmly convinced of the need for radical change. The bishops are quite aware that

> all of us need a profound conversion so that 'the kingdom of justice, love and peace' might come to us. ... We will not have a new continent without new and reformed structures, but, above all, there will be no new continent without new men, who know how to be truly free and responsible according to the light of the Gospel (no. 3).

In their call for "the construction of a new society" (no. 7) they demand radical social reforms which must include "an authentic and urgent reform of agrarian structures and policies." However, "this structural change and its political implications must go beyond a simple distribution of land." This will require "the organization of the peasants into effective intermediate structures, principally in the form of cooperatives" (no. 14). These are ideas for which a few years later one could be arrested, thrown into jail, and even tortured or killed as a "communist subversive" by the security forces in some Latin American countries.

The bishops heed the pope's warning against the danger of atheistic Marxism. They recognize the fact that Latin America at that time was caught between the forces of capitalism and communism. Defiantly they stake out a position between these two extremes, boldly declaring:

> The system of liberal capitalism and the temptation of the Marxist system would appear to exhaust the possibilities of transforming the economic structures of our continent. ... We must denounce the fact that Latin America sees itself caught between these two options and remains dependent on one or other of the centers of power which control its economy" (no. 10).

At the same time, however, they leave no doubt that Latin America has to liberate itself "from the neo-colonialism to which it is bound (no. 13).

The most penetrating statements coming out of Medellín are from the commission on Peace. Perhaps that is because Dom Hélder Câmara worked with this particular group. Here the bishops realistically observe the "power unjustly exercised by certain dominant sectors" that use "force to repress drastically any attempt at opposition," using the ideological excuse of anti-communism or the need to keep order "to give their action an honest appearance" (Medellín II, on Peace, no. 6).

Here the controversial statement on "institutionalized violence" is made. Without mincing words, the bishops declare: "Violence constitutes one of the gravest problems in Latin America" (no. 15). In other words, there is no realistic way to avoid violence. Violence is simply a fact of life in present-day Latin America. As the bishops articulate it in their document, "In many instances Latin America finds itself faced with a situation that can be called institutionalized violence" (no. 16). Thus the bishops urge the powerful and rich in their countries

> not to take advantage of the pacifist position of the Church in order to oppose, either actively or passively, the profound transformations that are so necessary. If they jealously retain their privileges, and defend them through violence they are responsible to history for provoking 'explosive revolutions of despair' (no. 17).

They even found support for this severe admonition in Pope Paul VI himself, who spoke of "explosive revolutions of despair" only a few days earlier in Bogotá. In his encyclica "Populorum Progressio" the pope had admitted that revolutionary insurrection can be legitimate in the case of evident and prolonged "tyranny that seriously works against the fundamental rights of man, and which damages the common good of the country." The bishops agreed with Paul VI, however, that "armed revolution generally generates new injustices, introduces new imbalances and causes new disasters: one cannot combat a real evil at the price of a greater evil" (no. 19).

To this Protestant observer, the bishops' statement on Family and Demography was one of the weakest documents from Medellín. In a wooden, uninspired manner it merely regurgitates the encyclica "Humanae Vitae":

> The teaching of the Magisterium forbidding the voluntary use of artificial means that thwart the conjugal act is clear and unmistakable" (Medellin II, on Family and Demography, no. 11).

Couples are to exercise self-control. In this way, it is hoped, the population bomb will not explode but be diffused. "Good luck!" I thought. I had pointed out on several occasions that a peaceful and orderly transformation of Latin America is impossible without the pill, but my warnings were angrily brushed aside as the comments of an outsider who did not understand the Latin American reality. Contraception was a pill the Roman Catholic Church was not ready to swallow. "Humanae Vitae" sat in the middle of the table at all the deliberations in Medellín, blocking any enlightened approach to the looming demographic crisis.

While this short-sighted attitude toward a reasonable planned parenthood has to be severely criticized, in other ways Medellín accomplished a spiritual breakthrough for Latin America. In the true spirit of the Second Vatican Council the bishops spoke out as authentic pastors for the people entrusted to their care, taking up their pressing needs and struggling to find concrete help for them. The prelates were fully aware that profound political and social transformation in Latin America is unavoidable if people are to have a better future.

For these church leaders, a renewal of their continent guided by God's Spirit means nothing less than a "new pentecost." Among other things, a new start will require the creation of new structures in the social makeup of their societies. This can happen only when there are "new people" genuinely set free through the gospel of Jesus Christ. The land with all its rich resources must be distributed in a new way; without agrarian reform the task will be impossible. The poor and disadvantaged must band together in new associations in order to have their voices heard. And finally, oppressive power by the rich and privileged must be taken away if institutionalized violence is to stop in Latin America.

IV
A CALL TO REPENTANCE

"We can no longer speak of one, unified Latin American horizon. Rather our real problems today are regional and local in nature." Willy Hansen, Professor for Systematic Theology, in a panel discussion at I.S.E.D.E.T. on July 16, 1998.

The bishops had come up with a strong, convincing message. Their statements may not always be smoothly coherent in every detail. But the reason for this can be found in the woeful fragmentation of a Latin America which presents a far from coherent face to the rest of the world. The message of Medellín could hardly be more cohesive than the context out of which it arose.

The bishops tried hard to stay within the limits that Pope Paul VI had set. They did an admirable job of juggling the three balls which the pontiff had pitched to them: keeping in touch with the social transformations of their continent, maintaining a posture of non-violence, and enforcing a total ban on artificial birth and population control.

But with all of their good intentions, the church leaders were on a Mission Impossible. This was quickly recognized by the liberation theologians, who saw the flaw in the attempted combination. The fundamental error was the bishops' underlying assumption that all of Latin America's deficiencies and needs could be overcome by a gradual development in the history of the human family. This was and is a hollow hope, false because it ignores the basic fact that Latin America does not enjoy a free and independent life of its own. Along with many other areas of the Third World, Latin America exists in political and economic dependence upon the First World, especially the United States and the countries of northern Europe.

With the publication of his *A Theology of Liberation* in 1971 (English translation 1973; the following citations are from the 1988 15th anniversary edition), Gustavo Gutiérrez becomes the first in a long line of liberation theologians. From the very beginning he rejects the concept of development and seeks to replace it with the more dynamic idea of liberation:

> The term *development* has synthesized the aspirations of poor peoples during the last few decades. Recently, however, it has become the object of severe criticism due both to the deficiencies of the development policies proposed to the poor countries to lead them out of their underdevelopment and also to the lack of concrete achievements of the interested governments. This is the reason why *developmentalism (desarrollismo)* ... is now used in a pejorative

sense, especially in Latin America (p. 16; all emphases are in Gutiérrez's original text).

This harsh rejection of development and developmentalism is still held today by most Latin American thinkers as something that has no real meaning in their specific context. The term liberation, on the other hand, stands for a historical process in which the hopes and aspirations of oppressed peoples and social classes can be met. The word development often gives "a false picture of a tragic and conflictual reality." But:

> At a deeper level, *liberation* can be applied to an understanding of history. Humankind is seen as assuming conscious responsibility for its own destiny. This understanding provides a dynamic context and broadens the horizons of the desired social changes (p. 24).

Gutiérrez is certain that he is supported by the biblical witness in this understanding. He asserts: "In the Bible, Christ is presented as the one who brings us liberation. ... Christ makes humankind truly free, that is to say, he enables us to live in communion with him; and this is the basis for all human fellowship" (p. 25).

In many respects, Latin American Liberation Theology is a clear call to repentance. It calls the church itself to repentance; for it is a church badly in need of renovation. Traditionally the Roman Catholic Church in Latin America has always been on the side of the rich and powerful. But now the Theology of Liberation seeks to free this church by taking her out of this position of privilege.

At the very beginning, the church was a close ally of the Spanish and Portuguese monarchs. It has always promoted the cross of Christ. But all too often the cross of Christ came to the peoples of this continent through the sword of the *conquistadores*. It was not always Christ alone who bled on the cross. Often the people upon whom the cross was laid were bleeding as well.

How much has changed through the centuries? Perhaps not that much. In our time as well, the church in Latin America has closely allied herself with the power brokers and dictators who subjugate and exploit the poor of that continent. As a result, the church has lived in a kind of protected ghetto sheltered from the harsh conditions of the broad masses.

The liberationists realize that the Roman Catholic Church in Latin America needs an awakening, a clear call to get up and leave its ghetto. But for this very reason the sharp contrast between development and liberation must be maintained. Gutiérrez observes correctly:

> The Latin American Church has lived and to a large extent continues to live as a ghetto church. The Latin American Christian community came into being during the Counter-Reformation and has always been characterized by its defensive attitude as regards the faith (p. 58).

As a child of the Counter-Reformation, the Catholic Church in Latin America never had a living connection with the Reformation of Martin Luther. Subsequent movements of liberation arising in the following centuries out of Luther's spiritual revolution remained for the most part a closed book to the Latin American church. The Age of Enlightenment seemed to pass her by. She felt ill at ease with the revolutions in America and France. So she simply sat pat like a stolid, musty old aristocrat, breathing in the stale air of inherited privilege.

Gutiérrez does not provide a detailed analysis on this point. But he observes:

> This posture was reinforced in some cases by the hostility of the liberal and anticlerical movements of the nineteenth century and, more recently, by strong criticism from those struggling to transform the society to which the Church is so tightly linked (ibid.).

Because of this cramped attitude, the Church had no alternative but to seek the support of economically powerful groups and to resist any change that could threaten the established order.

Thus the Church must turn around in a dramatic way. For Gutiérrez, the time has come to leave the sheltered ghetto. He tries to jolt her into a new awareness. He draws an unflattering comparison between the Second Vatican Council and the Bishops' Conference in Medellín:

> At Medellín, the Latin American Church, despite the climate created by the Eucharistic Congress held in Bogotá immediately before it, realistically perceived the world in which it was and clearly saw its place in that world. In short, it began to be aware of its own coming of age and to take the reins of its own destiny. Vatican II speaks of the underdevelopment of peoples, of the developed countries and what they can and should do about this underdevelopment; Medellín tries to deal with the problem from the standpoint of the poor countries, characterizing them as subjected to a new kind of colonialism. Vatican II talks about a Church in the world and describes the relationship in a way which tends to neutralize the conflicts; Medellín demonstrates that the world in which the Latin American Church ought to be present is in full revolution. Vatican II sketches a general outline for Church renewal; Medellín provides guidelines for a transformation of the Church in terms of its presence on a continent of misery and injustice"(p. 73).

These are revolutionary ideas. In their deliberations in Medellín the bishops had talked about the transformation of their church "in the light of the Vatican Council." The new program of liberation which is demanded by Gutiérrez could rightly be called "transforming the church in opposition to the Vatican Council."

The call to repentance as it is issued by Latin American Liberation Theology is rather a shout, an urgent cry to the Roman Catholic Church and especially its prelates to relinquish their positions of privilege alongside the rich and powerful, to find their place at the side of the oppressed and exploited peoples in their countries. In order to exercise their office as true shepherds, they must become the voice of the voiceless.

IV

It should be noted that to a large extent Liberation Theology in Latin America has been an internal debate within the Roman Catholic Church. This is a phenomenon of which an outside observer must continually be aware, whether the observer is non-Roman Catholic or non-Latin American. But having said that, it is frustrating to see how few Protestant sources are used by liberation theologians. Perhaps they are too eager to show their compliance with the teaching authority of the Church, or are unaware of earlier church reforms. But they have largely ignored the lasting contributions to church renewal by Martin Luther, John Calvin, the Wesley brothers and many others. Nevertheless, my irritation is lessened as I remind myself that in this debate one Roman Catholic is talking to another Roman Catholic.

Yet a heavy price must be paid in the long run for the provincialism that is at work here. This kind of myopic view breeds a narrow-mindedness that refuses to question the church's hierarchical party line, grounded in her arrogant claim to exclusive ownership of salvation that was once again reinforced in the declaration "Jesus Dominus" of 2000.

There can be no question about the strong commitment to liberation evidenced by many Latin American theologians. But most of them could not break out of the spiritual limits set by their church institution. Behind the facade of bold, radical demands they did not dare to plum the depths of the many problems and attack the evil at its spiritual roots. In the end they proved incapable of leading their community of faith out of her self-imposed ghetto.

Still, one must acknowledge that the call to repentance is honest. It is more than just the desperate shout of some liberation theologians. At Medellín the bishops, too, proved that they heard and understood this cry. As we have seen, at their conference they sounded their own call to repentance:

> We will not have a new continent without new and reformed structures, but above all, there will be no new continent without new men, who know how to be truly free and responsible according to the light of the Gospel. (Medellín II, on Justice, no. 3).

The Roman Catholic Church is still the most visible religious force in Latin America, and her call to repentance is directed first and foremost to herself. But no Christian community should consider itself exempt. All congregations, church bodies, and denominations are constantly tempted by the lure of wealth, privilege and power and must heed this call as well.

Latin America experiences the burden of power in the form of a dependency from which it cannot free itself. The idea that a gradual general development will bring relief is for Liberation Theology nothing but an illusion and must be rejected. Effective help can come only through the process of a genuine liberation. Gutiérrez dedicates a whole chapter to this discussion of liberation and development (*Theology*, pp. 13-25), and others take up the subject time and again, always rejecting development in the same unforgiving way. But buried within this debate lies an explosive charge. For the uninitiated, "liberation" and "development" may sound like innocuous terms. But in Latin America they are the external wrappings of a radical polarization.

Without exception, Latin American liberation theologians draw a line of separation that makes their call to repentance clear, credible and acceptable. The categories and images vary: free and slave, master and servant, independent and dependent, developed and underdeveloped, rich and poor, people living in an empire and people living in the colonies. All the above are expressions they use.

If a clear line of separation between liberation and development is not drawn by a responsible and relevant theology, or if the distinction is blurred, renewal becomes a sham or silly game. Then the act of repentance turns into a caricature—perpetrators of evil are bemoaned as victims, bullies mistaken for choir boys. The resulting inversion is as grotesque as the expectation that a condemned Jew should weep for the plight of the Nazi SS officer who must send him to the gas chamber. The real struggle is between oppressor and oppressed, exploiter and exploited, abuser and abused.

As we observed in chapter 2, a mood of hope existed at the end of the sixties and the beginning of the seventies. There was an underlying optimism that things can be changed for the better. In keeping with this positive outlook, a powerful biblical example suggested itself to Liberation Theology in the message of Exodus: We must break away from the land of slavery; we must leave behind the fleshpots of Egypt and set out on a long march through the wilderness in order to reach the promised land (Gutiérrez, *Theology*, pp. 88-89). This theme was repeated by liberation theologians in many variations. They saw an urgent need for a clear break with the past and a radically new start as in the biblical Exodus.

But when the Hebrew people left Egypt, there was no doubt about the enemy; it was Pharaoh who kept them in slavery. Thousands of years later, there was no doubt in the minds of the Jewish people who was the enemy; the Pharaoh of the twentieth century was Adolph Hitler who murdered them at Auschwitz. Unfortunately, such absolute clarity in naming the enemy was not granted to the Latin American liberationists.

They point to many culprits. They rightly condemn the mechanisms by which their societies are kept in a state of underdevelopment. They deplore the influence which the economically affluent and culturally dominant nations have over them. They rail against the colonial-like power exercised by the First World throughout the Third World. Certainly there is enough blame to go around. This writer can be accused of sharing the guilt of oppression on three accounts: he is white, male, and a U.S. citizen.

Yet as one digs for a clear, unambiguous answer, one receives a lot of evasive responses. In the end, it is not at all clear who must take the blame for the massive poverty and misery in Latin America. Is it the monarchs of Spain and Portugal, who gave to a few aristocrats the deed and title to vast territories in return for gold plundered from indigenous populations for the crown? Is it the conquistadores who colonized with the cross and the sword? Is it the rich and powerful elites in contemporary Latin America, who enjoy fabulous wealth while the masses live in squalor? Is it the capitalist businessmen from the North, who invest large sums in Latin America? Is it the International Monetary Fund, whose banks extend huge credits to Latin American governments without guarantee of repayment? Is it the Western diplomats, who negotiate weighted trade agreements between their own and Latin American countries?

Liberation Theology does not give a clear or convincing answer to these questions. Perhaps its spokesmen did not feel the need to do so. Perhaps that has not been its mandate or responsibility. In any case, the question of who is the Pharaoh in Latin America today is clearly not as easy to answer as it may have seemed to some along the way.

V
LATIN AMERICA FINDS A VOICE

"Liberation Theology attacked structural evil in society. That's what we urgently need. For the first time we had a real Latin American theology. Before that we only had some devotional literature that had grown in Latin America." Ricardo Pietrantonio, Professor of New Testament, in a panel discussion at I.S.E.D.E.T. on July 16, 1998.

Latin American Liberation Theology is above all contextual theology "rising out of the urgent problems of real life" (Juan Luis Segundo, *The Liberation of Theology,* p. 4). And it is a contextual theology that found an immediate response in Latin America.

In the creation story we are told that after Eve was fashioned, Adam enthusiastically exclaimed: "This at last is bone of my bones and flesh of my flesh" (Genesis 2:23). Many Latin American theologians responded to the call to repentance issued by their colleagues in the faith in a similar manner. They appeared to greet the appearance of the new theology with the shout: "This at last is bone of my bones and flesh of my flesh!"

It is not our intention to present here a compendium or even a summary of all the works that have been written on Latin American Liberation Theology. Such an attempt would exceed the limits of this study. But some examples of the movement should be shown. Although insufficient, they will give an idea of the rich contributions that have made this theology so important in Latin America.

1. Juan Luis Segundo: The Principle of Suspicion
The Liberation of Theology. Maryknoll, NY, Orbis Books, 1976 [Spanish edition appeared in 1975].

The ideas of this Uruguayan Jesuit theologian, who died in 1996, are already somewhat familiar to us. However, it is still necessary to explain the particular basic thrust of his work. He intends to equip Latin American Liberation Theology with a distinct methodology, and to this end he develops his "hermeneutical circle" (pp. 7-38).

The concept of such a circle is not new. It was used by Rudolf Bultmann in his interpretation of the Bible. This German scholar was a Lutheran. Using a unique pattern he continued Luther's basic approach to the scriptures of interpreting the bible from its central message, namely the gospel of Jesus Christ. Bultmann pushed this approach to a new level through a program of demythologization by which he distinguished the central message (kerygma) from ancient myths. He described the encounter of modern man with the scriptures of the Old and New Testament in a circular fashion. When modern man is confronted with the ancient texts, he finds a split in what these texts actually say. On the one hand, there are elements of an outdated world view, such as a three-tiered universe or a creation in seven days, which Bultmann called myths. On the other hand, there is a kerygma, a clear message which still speaks to the modern reader and gives him a new sense of direction. While he often feels at first confused by the old biblical texts, after putting aside the "mythical" elements he gets a grip on the central message and comes to a new encounter with the bible as God's living Word. In this way the circle of understanding becomes complete.

Segundo applies the idea of a hermeneutical circle to the situation in Latin America, and in the process he comes up with some radical changes. In place of Bultmann's existentialist self-understanding felt by modern man in Paris, London, Rome, or Berlin, Segundo starts from a different point. For him it is the collective experience of a given reality that is important as a foundation for understanding, rather than the subjective perception of a single person. One may call this a distinctly Latin American perspective; what matters for Segundo is not one's individual experience but the collective reality felt by the great majority of his fellow Latin Americans. Where collective experience is laid as a foundation, a completely different circle of understanding comes into play.

Segundo explains the four decisive elements of his hermeneutical circle thus: 1) Our way of experiencing reality brings us to an "ideological suspicion" about our real situation; 2) We apply this ideological suspicion to the whole ideological superstructure in general and to theology in particular; 3) We are led to the new suspicion that current biblical interpretation does not take all the relevant data into account; 4) We have our new hermeneutics, i.e. a new way of interpreting the Scripture, with the new elements at our disposal (p. 9).

One may question whether it is legitimate to elevate suspicion to the point of becoming a principle for interpreting the bible. But this is a suspicion that is fully justified. If you live in a situation in which violence has been institutionalized, in which hunger and deprivation are the daily norm and you are constantly exploited by one force or another, reason requires you to be paranoid. Then you will look upon different forms of interpreting the bible with a basic mistrust. At the same time you may discover in the biblical narratives people like yourself who were fellow sufferers, ignored and exploited by their powerful and wealthy in a similar fashion. New insights into the central message of our common "fountainhead of the faith" (ibid.) are bound to open up. This is the new hermeneutical circle devised by Segundo from a Latin American perspective.

2. José Porfirio Miranda: The Radical Love of the Bible
Marx and the Bible—A Critique of the Philosophy of Oppression. Maryknoll, New York: Orbis Books, 1974 [Spanish edition appeared in 1971].

Miranda is a Mexican priest. His book originally appeared in the same year as Peruvian priest Gustavo Gutiérrez's *A Theology of Liberation*. While Miranda makes it quite clear that his convictions are Christian, not Marxist, as a serious biblical scholar he develops a scathing critique of Western culture and its undergirding classical Greek philosophy.

Based primarily on the work of German exegetes of the Old and New Testament such as Gerhard von Rad, Walther Zimmerli, Otto Michel, Otto Kuss, Paul Althaus, and Rudolf Bultmann, Miranda shows the incompatability between the abstract logic of Greek philosophy and the concreteness of biblical thought. Although Christian theology is deeply indebted to the classical philosophers and has extensively used their categories for the systematization of its own concepts—a fact Miranda recognizes—he leaves no doubt that the Greek idea of private property and private ownership of the means of production are at the root of all the oppression inflicted by man upon man through the centuries. Capitalism is but the last link in a long chain of enslavement:

> And the root existed long before its capitalistic manifestation, long before it generated the present all-pervading and self-justifying system which enslaves man's id, ego, and superego—in the oppressor as much as or more than in the oppressed (p. xviii).

Miranda"s intention is not "to find parallels between the Bible and Marx, but rather simply to understand the Bible" (p. xvii). But in reading his Bible, he discovers that Karl Marx's "passion for justice originated in the Bible" (ibid.)

Against the capitalist values of Western culture Miranda summons the God of the Old and New Testament. He proves to be an authentic theologian: His concern is with the encounter between man and the living God. In scripture he finds a God who is different from the one whose image is widespread in Western culture. One has to make a decision either for God or for a false idol. "What is at the bottom of all this is a different God," he writes (p. 60). Yahweh, the God of Jeremiah, Hosea, Habakkuk, and Isaiah who can be "known" only by those who do justice is the same God who is "known" by everyone who loves (ibid.), as is so eloquently expressed by John in his letter: "Anyone who fails to love has not known God, because God is love" (1 John 4:7-8).

Miranda clearly understands the intention of John. "God is knowable only through one's neighbor," he says (p. 64). God is always radically "the Other." This is quite different from the dominant view in Western culture. He observes:

> In the Greco-Western approach to knowledge, the other and the others can disappear once they have fulfilled their informative or instructive task. ... In contrast, the God of the Bible must always be present as the Other. ...The God of the Bible does not affect us as something which must be overcome, encompassed, dominated, but independently of us, as the one who, beyond any relationship which we can establish with him, reappears as absolute (p. 65f).

The classical Greeks gave us the methods to develop our science. But science

> neutralizes reality. It was born to 'objectify' reality. And from the beginning it constitutes an aristocratic wisdom for free privileged people in the midst of a population of which five-sixths were slaves. Aristotle sums it all up in his classic thesis: Truth is incompatible with the condition of the slave" (p. 262).

Greek wisdom then allows us to contemplate reality. But in sharp contrast, "knowing" as it is presented in the Bible demands of us a definite "doing," it demands praxis, the actual doing of justice and love. "Biblical knowledge demands praxis to the point of being identified with it" (p. 266).

But the same demand of praxis is also made by Marx in his struggle for justice. This is accepted by Miranda as a clear challenge for the Christian believer:

> As Christians we really have to choose. The Marxist hope is that the world be transformed when the relationships among men become true bonds of love and justice. If this seems utopian to the Western intellect, what must this intellect think of biblical hope, which expects exactly the same thing, but also includes in the transformation of the world nothing less than the resurrection of the dead—something which Marx did not have the dialectic sufficient to reach? (p. 277).

With this emphasis upon action and praxis Miranda joins hands with his theological counterpart Gustavo Gutiérrez. For Gutiérrez, this is the firm foundation on which any theological reflection must be built. Since the Christian community professes "a faith active in love," the first step always has to be "real charity, action, and commitment to the service of others." Theology as a reflection and as a critical attitude must be the second step. It always follows, it does not lead the way. "It only rises at sundown," Gutiérrez writes, paraphrasing Hegel, and he continues:

> Theology does not produce pastoral activity; rather it reflects upon it. Theology must be able to find in pastoral activity the presence of the Spirit inspiring the action of the Christian community (Gutiérrez, *Theology*, p. 9).

3. Leonardo Boff, O.F.M.: A Voice for the Voiceless
Jesus Christ Liberator—A Critical Christology for Our Time, Maryknoll, New York: Orbis Books, 1978 [Portuguese edition appeared in 1972].

Boff, a Brazilian, was a Franciscan at the time he wrote this book but has since left the priesthood. The bibliography for his *Christology* shows that he was educated in Germany; nearly all of the German theological luminaries seem to have found a place in his footnotes. But Boff warns his readers:

> The predominantly foreign literature that we cite ought not to delude anyone. It is with preoccupations that are ours alone, taken from our Latin American context, that we will reread not only the old texts of the New Testament but also the most recent commentaries written in Europe (p. 43).

Boff is very much a Latin American. As such he observes: "Our sky possesses different stars that form different figures of the zodiac by which we orient ourselves in the adventures of faith and of life" (ibid.).

In order to speak to the people of our time the church must begin with

Christology. It is not enough simply to repeat the traditional doctrine about Christ. Rather, the message of faith has to be critically thought through in a new way in order to be still credible today. With this concern Boff shows a great similarity with Martin Luther. Luther, a former Augustinian monk, developed his theology of the cross by putting a special emphasis on the human nature of Christ and particularly his wounds. Boff, at that time still a Franciscan, presents a theology which finds its center in the incarnation. In a very similar fashion he also puts a great emphasis on the humanity of Christ:

> Therefore the Incarnation contains a message that concern not only Jesus Christ but also the nature and destiny of every person. By means of the Incarnation we come to know who in fact we are and what we are destined for. We come to know the nature of God, who in Jesus Christ comes to our encounter with a face like ours—respecting our otherness—in order to assume human nature and fill it with his divine reality (p. 205).

Boff sets out five distinctive marks of a typical Latin American Christology:

1.) *The Primacy of the Anthropological Element over the Ecclesiastical.*
In a highly provocative manner he declares that in today's Latin America "the special focus is not so much the church but the human person that it should help, raise up, and humanize." He maintains that "in Latin American theological thought, there reigns an accentuated scepticism" over against "models and structures imported from Europe." Here we have again Segundo's principle of a Latin American suspicion. Only this time it is directed against a "dogmatically interpreted canon law and juridically interpreted dogma" (p. 44).

2.) *The Primacy of the Utopian Element over the Factual.*
For the Latin American person the determining element is not the past but the future since the past was dominated by the European colonizers. This is why "utopia" is such an important element in the construction of a meaningful future. Here utopia is understood not in the sense of escaping into some illusion, but as a source of hope. This is how faith in Christ is lived out today. "Faith promises and demonstrates as realized in Christ a utopia that consists in a world totally reconciled, a world that is the fulfilment of what we are creating here on earth with feeling and love" (ibid.).

3.) *The Primacy of the Critical Element over the Dogmatic.*
Many church traditions and institutions have served well in the past. But today they have become obsolete and destructive since they lock "the door to a dialogue between faith and the world, the church and society. Criticism refines and purifies the core of the Christian experience so that it can be made incarnate within the historical experience we are living" (p. 45).

4.) *The Primacy of the Social over the Personal.*
Immense portions of the Latin American population are living on the edge of

society. Therefore raising the issue of conversion primarily in personal terms is hopelessly inadequate. "There are structural evils that transcend individual ones." The church therefore cannot be content with creating "its own little world within the great world. Like Jesus, it ought to give special attention to the nobodies and those without a voice" (p. 46).

5.) *The Primacy of Orthopraxis over Orthodoxy.*

Although the church always preached Christ the liberator, the church itself did not actually liberate or actively support liberation movements. Boff therefore underscores the element which is constitutive for all Liberation Theologies in Latin America, and this is the demand of orthopraxis. We have already seen that Miranda insisted that only by doing the right thing one can really "know" God. Miranda demanded a clear praxis of the Christian faith. Similarly, Gutiérrez laid down the life, preaching, and historical commitment of the Church as the foundation for any theological reflection.

In the same spirit Boff now points out the serious flaws in classical Christology:

> The fundamental theme of the Synoptic Gospels, on following Christ, has been poorly thematized and translated into concrete attitudes. Orthodoxy, that is correct thinking about Christ occupied primacy over orthopraxis, correct acting in the light of Christ. ... Not rarely the church has left active, participating Christians as complete orphans. This has resulted in recent years in the continuous exodus from the church of the best minds and most active forces (pp. 44-47).

Just like Miranda and Gutiérrez, Boff demands the "praxiological moment" of the message of Christ (ibid.). Following in the footsteps of the great medieval Franciscan John Duns Scotus, he maintains that "we are all destined to be images and likenesses of Jesus Christ" (p. 204). Boff is fully confident that "through love we can open ourselves in such a way to God and others that we completely empty ourselves and fill ourselves in the same proportion with the reality of others and God" (p. 205).

Boff advances theses which are revolutionary for a Franciscan loyal to his church. They got him into trouble not only with the hierarchy but with the security forces of his government. In a preface and an epilogue which were added six years later, the reader is alerted to the fact that Boff's original Christology was published in 1972 at a time of severe political repression. He explains: "The word 'liberation' was forbidden to be used in all the communications media." Although he could not express himself as freely as he wanted, "the liberation message was understood by Christians." His hope is

> that the reading of this book will help more privileged Christians to join in fellowship with those who are more oppressed, to commit themselves to the messianic task of liberating human beings completely from everything that diminishes them and offends God (p. xii).

4. Jon Sobrino, S.J.: In the Footsteps of the Historical Jesus

Christology at the Crossroads—A Latin American Approach, Maryknoll, New York: Orbis Books, 1978. [Spanish edition appeared in 1976.]

Sobrino is a Jesuit priest and professor in El Salvador. In November 1989 he survived the massacre of seven fellow Jesuits at his university because he was abroad at the time. He holds an engineering degree from St. Louis University and a doctorate in theology from the Hochschule Sankt Georgen in Frankfurt, Germany. Like Boff he is well versed in the latest achievements of German theologians. He appreciates the outstanding contribution of his Latin American colleague. But he also feels he can add to it as he recognizes that "for the most part Latin Americans have not worked out systematic Christologies and full presentations of Christ" (p. 33).

In the same way as the Brazilian Franciscan Boff, this Jesuit from El Salvador argues for a new approach to Christology which puts greater emphasis on the historical Jesus and his life of service to the poor than on the Christ of church dogma. He sees the church standing at a crossroads at the present time. His aim is

> to show how forgetfulness of the historical Jesus and one-sided concentration on the risen Christ has in fact led Christian faith to take on a religious structure in the pejorative sense (p. 277).

There is a great tension between Christian faith and natural religion. In "religion" God is already defined and determined in his characteristics of omnipotence, omniscience, and retributive justice. But in Christian faith God "appears in a very specific context, namely, when he 'hears the cries of the oppressed'" (p. 276). Therefore we cannot talk about the meaning of the world or of history as long as injustice and the cries of the oppressed continue. Christian faith has been shaped by a completely different image of God:

> The Christian God does not guarantee our security through any legalistic mechanism. He guarantees it in a most paradoxical way, demanding that we give up all our security and abandon ourselves to God. We see this in the Bible when Abraham is asked to leave his father's house and live solely by hope (ibid.).

Sobrino lists some of the strong tensions which exist in the church today: tension between Faith and Religion, between Jesus of Nazareth and the Spirit of the Risen Lord, between Faith and an Explicative, Metaphysical Theology, between Prophetic Political Theology and Power-Centered Political Theology, and between Cultic Worship and Concrete Discipleship (pp. 273-304; the capitalizations are Sobrino's). These are not mutually exclusive, either-or comparrisons or dimensions. But Sobrino insists that we clarify our priorities and determine what comes first and what second (p. 275).

For Sobrino the overriding question is: What is the correct way to gain access to Christ? His answer is that we gain access to the Christ of faith, the resurrected Lord, through a direct intentional act such as a profession of faith, a doxology, or cultic worship. However we gain access to the historical Jesus through one way only, as the Gospel make clear: "We gain access to him only through a specific kind of praxis, which the Gospels describe as the 'following of Jesus' or 'discipleship.'" Therefore our own priority today has to lie with the historical Jesus. "Access to the Christ of faith can only come through access to the historical Jesus, through discipleship" (ibid.).

5. Enrique Dussel: Land of the Conqueror and Conquered
History and the Theology of Liberation, Maryknoll, New York: Orbis Books, 1976. [Spanish edition appeared in 1975.]

An Argentine historian with a doctorate in philosophy from Madrid and in history from the Sorbonne, Dussel also studied with the Roman Catholic Reformation scholar Joseph Lortz in Mainz, Germany. He was still in his native Argentina when he delivered these lectures and later published them in book form. Under pressure from the military dictatorship he fled his country and settled in Mexico. In recent years he has explored the relationship of African and Latin American philosophies and promoted the importance of symbols, rites, music, images and stories to an authentic, living Latin American Church.

In his book Dussel wants to fill a vacuum which is keenly felt by many Latin Americans. He intends to give them a history of their own. "We as Latin Americans are 'outside history', he writes (p. 12); for there is no written history of Latin American culture that is worth anything. "If we want to train people, we send them to Europe," he observes with biting irony, and continues:

> When they come back, they are completely lost in Latin America. They are out of touch and never get their feet back on the ground. They are Frenchified, Germanized, Italianized, or otherwise alienated (p. 18).

"From the start" means for a Latin American "beginning in 1492." The discovery of Columbus is the birth of the American continent. As Dussel points out, "our mother is Amerindia, our father is Spain—or vice versa, if you will. But the child of this union is something new. ... It is a new culture, a mixed culture, a Creole or mestizo culture" (p. 32). In tracing Latin America's own history Dussel goes into a very detailed discussion both of the Aztec and the Inca world view that is a part of its heritage to this day.

Like the rest of his fellow liberationists, Dussel is convinced that the Latin American reality can be understood only when the Latin part of the continent (i.e., for Latin Americans North, Central and South America are considered one continent) is viewed as a dependent and oppressed area. As he tells the story of Latin America, he describes how it was first dominated by Spain:

> Spain dominated our colonial version of Christendom. It took our gold and silver to finance its operations against German Lutherans. And this gold and silver was obtained from the blood of our native Indians. Tainted with the injustice in effect here, the Catholic rulers and their administrators pleaded

for money to carry out the great Catholic crusade against 'the Lutheran heretics.' Latin America lived within the totality of Spanish culture—aware of its underdeveloped situation and of its powerlessness. Its people were 'oppressed' (p. 99).

Ever since, Latin America has not been able to break out of this circle of injustice, powerlessness, and violence. Even when different Latin American countries rebelled against their colonial masters and broke away from them, they did not really achieve true independence. Their native Creole elites merely switched their allegiance from one superpower to another, from Spain to England and later to other powers:

> Spain had taken gold and silver from Latin America and had offered wine and oil in return—even though these could be produced here. England, by contrast, offered manufactured products in return for our raw materials—under the basic system spelled out by Adam Smith. This new arrangement was agreed upon by our Creole oligarchy. Our 'independence' was merely a switch from Spanish domination to domination by the new world power: industrial England. And our Creole oligarchy would take over the task of dominating people here (p. 100).

Dussel when writing his book still had high hopes that in our times things could radically change for the better. He felt sure that the poor people of Latin America were awakening to their situation and were about to trigger a revolutionary process that would lead to a "liberation of the whole Latin American people from the dominance of foreign empires" (ibid.). We now know that this hope did not come true. The great revolution never happened.

In narrating the Latin American story, Dussel does not forget to mention the long list of Christian martyrs. They stretch from a little-known Bishop Antonio de Valdivieso of Central America, who was assassinated for his persistent defense of the Indians in 1550 by the governor of Nicaragua (p. 97), to Henrique Pereira Neto, a young priest in Olinda and Recife who was killed by a commando of the Brazilian army on May 27, 1969 for his work among university students (p. 119), and on to Hector Gallegos of Panama, killed for his work with peasant cooperatives (p. 124f).

There is another well-known Latin American martyr. Camilo Torres was a priest and sociologist in Colombia. During that country's never-ending civil war he joined the resistance as chaplain to the guerrillas and was killed. Dussel points out: "We do not know for sure whether he died as a guerrilla fighter, or whether he was assassinated first and then passed off as such" (p. 124). This method of assassination was increasingly practised in subsequent years by the security forces of the Latin American dictatorships as a convenient cover for their murders.

Torres had come to the conclusion that a revolution was necessary if the hungry were to be fed, the naked clothed, and well-being brought to the majority of people. He was ready to take the risks that such an ideal would demand. As Dussel reports, four months before his death the young Colombian priest while expressing his admiration for dedicated Marxists declared that he was not one of them when he made this confession:

> They are sincerely seeking the truth and they love their neighbor in an efficacacious way, but they must know very well that I will never enter their ranks. I will never be a communist—neither as a Colombian, a sociologist, a Christian, or a priest (p. 123).

Communist or not, Torres died as a subversive rebel. But he inspired a great many with his example of completely dedicated love. A good portion of this same spirit also rubbed off on Dussel, who shared the same admiration for committed Marxists without being one himself.

At that time Dussel was dreaming along with all the other liberation theologians of the possibility of bringing some form of socialism to Latin America as the principal cure for most of its major problems. "We seem to be moving towards more serious consideration of socialism," he cautiously explained, even if it was not necessarily a Marxist version (p. 135f). In this hope he felt encouraged by a considerable number of leading bishops such as Hélder Câmara of Brazil and Sergio Méndez Arceo of Mexico. He was even able to quote a strong statement along these lines made by the bishops of Peru at their 1971 Synod:

> Christians ought to opt for socialism. We do not mean a bureaucratic, totalitarian, or atheistic socialism; we mean a socialism that is both humanistic and Christian (p. 134).

An indisputable invention of the Latin American Church is the formation of grass roots communities—*comunidades de base*. Dussel explains that they actually grew out of the Movement for Basic Education in Brazil. They have now become one of the basic building blocks for creating a church community particularly in large urban centers. As Dussel sees it,

> The individual living in urban Christendom is a lonely figure lost in a huge impersonal crowd. When he goes to Church, he often does not know the people on either side of him. There is no intermediary between the concrete individual and the impersonal Church. Something is needed to bridge the gap between the two, and that is what the 'basic community' seeks to do. It is a small community in which the participants render each other concrete help and thus empirically experience their fellowship with one another. The impersonal parish community at Sunday Mass is to be transformed into a collection of many such basic communities (p. 131).

This description gives one a feeling for the faceless multitudes who crowd into the metropolitan centers of Latin America from the countryside. Those who live in Europe or North America may not be familiar with the kind of atmosphere that surrounds the Latin American faithful in their packed, impersonal religious sanctuaries. As ministry is increasingly done in small groups, the grass roots communities of Latin American liberation Christians can serve as a helpful model. Dussel goes even so far as to make the claim "that we cannot really be part of the living Church nowadays without being a member of such a community" (p. 166).

6. Summary

What has been presented above is far from a full discussion of Liberation Theology. These five examples do not do justice even to the authors who are included; they are merely snapshots.

Several others deserve special mention, however. So far we have discussed only the work of Roman Catholic thinkers. Among the Protestants who have made significant contributions to the theme of liberation in Latin America are Rubem A. Alves, José Míguez Bonino, Julio de Santa Ana, and Arturo Blatezky. The close relationship between Christians and Marxists is explored in great detail by Hugo Assmann in his *Teología desde la praxis de la liberación* (1973).

It is hoped that the five theologians described here in some detail will give an insight into the broad wealth of ideas that has been generated by Liberation Theology. As we shall discuss at length in the final chapter, the movement is not without serious shortcomings. But it is important to highlight the enormous contributions made by this theological enterprise, summarized in the following seven points:

1.) The hallmark of this liberation movement is a one-sided partisanship toward the poor. There can be no theology of liberation without a clear commitment to those who are politically marginalized and economically exploited. This emphasis provides a particular focus for the reading of the bible. It is the poor to whom the good news of Jesus is directed in the first place. They are the ones who are to be saved by the Messiah before all others. For the liberation theologians this is the biblical core from which all other parts of the scripture are to be interpreted.

2.) From their situation in a dependent and oppressed Latin America, these theologians add an ideological component to the traditional critical methods of interpreting the bible. This is the principle of ideological suspicion intoduced by Juan Luis Segundo. It is to be used along with the other exegetical tools of text criticism, form criticism and redaction criticism. The ancient scriptural texts were influenced by the political and economic considerations of their times in the same way as is true of modern literature today. This must be taken into account in order to break through to the living message of the biblical narratives.

3.) Doing the right thing is more important than teaching the right thing. By far the strongest contribution Latin American Liberation Theology made is its insistence on the primacy of orthopraxis over orthodoxy. We have seen this demand particularly in Gutiérrez and Miranda, but it is made by all the liberation theologians. Without any doubt it is the most theologically controversial and divisive issue. We shall bring a more detailed discussion of this point later.

"Doing the right thing" is precisely what a great many people today look for in a community of faith. They often feel alienated from the Church because it does not fulfill this expectation. Orthopraxis means "walking the walk before talking the talk." This is certainly more complicated than it appears on the surface. But if the Christian Church wants to attract new and committed members in our secular world today she will have to be credible. She will have to get rid of empty words. She must learn how to transcend mere lip service when preaching love of one's neighbor and our common humanity.

4.) Intimately linked to the demand of "doing the right thing" is the basic Liberation Theology principle that concrete experiences of "faith, hope, and love" come first and theological reflection comes only afterwards. In this concept, concrete experience is the firm foundation. This means a complete break with the idea that there are eternal truths into which human experience must be forcibly pressed.

Miranda relentlessly opposes the truths that dominate classical Greek philosophy. It reminds us of Luther's break with the philosophical underpinnings of medieval theology in the Church of his time. There is also a refreshing touch of Luther in Miranda's concept of God coming to us "from outside ourselves," *extra nos*, as the One who is radically Other. And we hear an echo of Bonhoeffer's "Church for the Other" in Miranda's rejection of Aristotelian categories. He insists that the Church is built on the foundation not of unchanging eternal truths but of actually lived human experience.

5.) Concrete discipleship is yet another dimension of the demand for "doing the right thing" or orthopraxis. Boff and Sobrino develop this concept in their Christologies. As "good Catholics" they respect the confession of the early Church in 451 C.E. at the synod of Chalcedon that in Christ the two natures of being "fully God" and "fully human" are joined in an inseparable unity. But they place a greater emphasis on the historical Jesus and his life here on earth. He is served by discipleship through a ministry of concrete love to one's neighbor. The risen Christ who can be comprehended only by faith, on the other hand, is not given the same strong emphasis.

In our present times there are many people who have serious difficulty with the credal formulations of the Christian faith. They ask: "What does all this mean for my own life?" They can find a convincing answer in the advice of these Latin American theologians: You are called to follow in the footsteps of Jesus and become his disciples! You are destined to be images and likenesses of the historical Jesus!

6.) Latin American Liberation Theology wants to strike at the structural evil in modern life. This is rarely done by European or North American theologians. The Latin Americans try to reach the sin that is deeply imbedded in the fabric of society. They adamantly reject the notion of a gradual upward development in human history. They expected a radical revolution in the social structures of their countries, and they awaited the arrival of a new socialist order. As we have seen, most of them were not convinced Marxists themselves. But all of them hoped and fought for the coming of a humanistic, non-bureaucratic "socialism with a human face."

They were disappointed in that hope. As we know in hindsight, history took a different path. In a similar manner the first Christians were frustrated in their hope that the Second Coming of Christ would take place within their lifetime. When this event did not materialize, it was an embarrassing disappointment for some of them. Nevertheless, subsequent generations of believers did not give up their expectation of the Second Coming of their Lord. The liberationists in Latin America miscalculated in their hope of an imminent great revolution. It is an issue that they still must work through and come to terms with. But that does not invalidate the rich contributions of their theological movement. They can still find a reason to hope for social transformation and a new ordering of human affairs in Latin America.

7.) A legacy of Latin American church life that will enrich us all for a long time is their gift of grass roots communities. The *comunidades de base* "represent a major trend in the pastoral work of the future" as Enrique Dussel points out (Dussel, *History and Theology*, p. 131). This is true not only for Latin America but for Christian life wherever people are concentrated, especially in our "supercities." Such communities do not need to disrupt the larger context of the Church. With the impersonal nature of much of our contemporary life the grass roots communities provide believers with a concrete fellowship where they can learn from each other how to follow in the footsteps of Jesus. Here they can practise love in service to their fellow humanity.

VI
THE REVOLUTION THAT NEVER CAME

"The trouble with Liberation Theology was that it was exclusively socialist in orientation. That made it almost impossible to have a discussion with those of a different political persuasion." Pablo Andiñach, Professor of Old Testament, in a panel discussion at I.S.E.D.E.T. on July 16, 1998.

In August 1975 I attended a conference in Detroit called "Theology in the Americas." The first of its kind, it was an encounter between liberation theologians from North America and Latin America. Although many of the attendees were friends, colleagues, and comrades, they held differing views and clashed passionately against each other in a real encounter that at times became quite overheated.

Most of the prominent Latin American leaders in Liberation Theology were there. North America was represented by well-known Black theologians such as James H. Cone and Cornell West whose impeccable credentials had been won in the civil rights struggle. In addition there were North American leaders of Native American tribes with their distinctive brand of theology, and members of a new theological group that had recently appeared on the scene—feminists, whose struggle had been given little serious attention until recently. In Detroit these women could speak with force and conviction about their own oppression and enslavement.

The Detroit conference was a colorful mix indeed. But the Latin American delegation dominated the event. It seemed to offer the clearest and most united front. As one observer remarked:

> The conference revealed that North Americans do not yet agree on a single approach to an understanding of the social realities of the United States. Blacks spoke for a racist analysis, women spoke about sexism and others of economic imperialism (Thomas C. Fox, "Liberation Theology Tests U.S. Conscience," In *National Catholic Reporter* (September 5, 1975), p. 1— quoted in Hugo Assmann, *Theology for a Nomad Church,* p. 11).

By contrast, Frederick Herzog of Duke University Divinity School in North Carolina observed:

> In Detroit for the first time Latin American liberation theologians as a group expounded their position as a seemingly monolithic perspective to a North

American audience (ibid., p. 15).

At one point a sharp disagreement developed between Hugo Assmann and Frederick Herzog. Assmann leapt to the microphone and impatiently exploded: "Your North American theology is God's action in history without going through history" (ibid., p.16).

In spite of its Latin American emphasis, the Detroit conference brought together and highlighted three basic conflicts against which Christians had struggled for most of the late 20th century: division by race, division by sex, and class warfare. Initially some of the veteran civil rights fighters from the northern hemisphere as well as the old class warriors from the southern seemed puzzled by the occasionally strident noises coming from the feminists. They may well have wondered in their hearts if the complaints of these women were just the latest outbursts of a frivolous bourgeois culture. But in the end it all came together. Race, sex, and class discrimination are all evils which still tear at our cultures. Often it seems that progress in these three areas is painfully slow. The Latin Americans in Detroit reminded us that we are one in Christ.

1975 was the high point for Latin American Liberation Theology. Its light shone bright and clear at the Conference of the Americas in Detroit. It was also a time of intense literary activity. One book after another rolled off the presses, and many of them were soon translated into the major languages of the world.

But at the same time, sinister clouds were forming on the horizon, threatening the survival of this bold theological experiment. The first deadly blow would be dealt by the political powers in Latin America. The second would come from the teaching authority of the Catholic Church in Rome.

On September 11, 1973, General Augusto Pinochet staged a bloody coup d'état in Chile, overthrowing the democratically elected Marxist President Salvador Allende. This was not the first time that a group of generals decided to take the reins of a Latin American country into their hands. There had been plenty of military golpes before. But what was initiated now in Chile differed in the heightened degree of ferocity and bestiality.

Hearing the news of this overthrow, I remembered the day seven years earlier in June 1966 in Argentina when a group of generals deposed the elected President Arturo Illia. They simply surrounded the Casa Rosada in Buenos Aires with army tanks and informed the country's president that his time was up. Illia at first protested, and then simply took his coat and left his office.

But now in 1973 there were no longer any gentlemanly niceties. President Allende died in the Chilean coup. The propaganda machine for the new government claimed he had committed suicide, but few people bought this line. What followed was a merciless reign of terror that quickly spread to other countries. In 1975 military dictatorships took over in Brazil and Uruguay. In 1976 the generals once again seized power in Argentina, this time establishing an absolutely ruthless control over the people. When I made a short visit to Buenos Aires shortly before Easter that year, I felt as if I were in a country occupied by a brutal enemy, so terrified were the Argentine people of their own rulers. But that was just the beginning. In the years to come their suffering would become even worse. This movement of oppressive governments continued to spread throughout the continent until there was hardly a Latin American country that was not dominated by military force.

What in hindsight seems incredible is the degree to which the different adherents of Liberation Theology found themselves totally unprepared for these developments. They simply did not think that the history of the human race could move in such a direction. Their naiveté is puzzling and more than a bit curious, especially because many liberation theologians quoted the statement by Santayana: "Those who cannot remember the past are condemned to repeat it." On this point their understanding of history had failed them.

The only explanation that comes to mind is the fact that most liberation theologians firmly believed that human history would run in the opposite direction. Gustavo Gutiérrez had defined liberation as "the inescapable moment of radical change which is foreign to the ordinary use of the term *development*" (Gutiérrez, *Theology of Liberation*, p. 17; all emphases are Gutiérrez's). For him, the Church was "caught in a pincer-like movement" of two forces moving in the same direction:

> We are faced on the one hand with the affirmation of an ever more autonomous world, not religious, or in more positive terms, a world come of age. On the other hand we are also faced with this single vocation to salvation which values human history in Christian terms, although in a way different from that of the past (p. 46).

In this envisioned course of history there was apparently no provision for the return of the horrors of fascism. Nazism was a thing of the past. The future had to open up for some form of socialism. Or so it seemed to them. Liberation meant for Gutiérrez "in a deeper sense to see the becoming of humankind as a process of human emancipation in history." And that called for "the building up of *a new humanity*" (p. 56).

But what now unfolded in Latin America was in many respects equal to the inhumanities of the Nazis. To be sure, there was no systematic genocide of the Jews. To be sure, the number of victims in Latin America paled beside the enormous slaughter of the millions killed by the Nazis. Latin America did not produce a monster like Adolph Hitler; the holocaust in Europe is simply without comparison. However, in their fanaticism the Latin American generals were not far behind. In the abhorrence over the cruelties visited upon the Jewish people, the fact that the driving force motivating the Nazis was an insane hatred of communism is often overlooked or played down. Right up to the end of World War II, train locomotives in Germany often carried the inspirational motto: *"Sieg oder Bolschewistisches Chaos!"* ("Victory or Bolshevist Chaos!"). The message was clear: We must fight the communist evil to the bitter end!

The same panic fear of communism now raged unchecked in Latin America. All those considered subversive were arrested. Among them were many priests and Christian lay people. Some had made common cause with Marxist groups, others with peasant or student organizations. The military's purpose was clear: alleged enemies of the state had to be exterminated at all costs, even if innocent victims were hurt in the process. Concentration camps, detention centers and torture chambers sprang up all over the continent. Death squads roamed with impunity in many areas. Many of those human butchers competed among themselves to see who could devise the best torture for political prisoners without leaving any marks on their victims' bodies.

Some unfortunate detainees were flown in military planes over the ocean and then, drugged but still alive, unceremoniously dumped to their death in the waters below. Others found their end in fields in mass graves. Not all of the bodies have been recovered or identified. Elisabeth Käsemann, the daughter of this writer's former New Testament professor in Göttingen Ernst Käsemann, was murdered in one of the "cleansing actions" of 1977. She was 30 years old and lived with a student from I.S.E.D.E.T in Buenos Aires. Although she was innocent of any political crime, her boyfriend was supposedly linked to an underground group and that proved to be her undoing.

The babies of young women who gave birth in detention centers were taken from their mothers and given or sold to rich childless couples for adoption. In Argentina between 1976 and 1982 an estimated 30,000 persons disappeared without a trace under the regime of Lieutenant General Jorge Videla. These *desaparecidos* are mourned by their mothers and grandmothers who have assembled every Thursday afternoon in white kerchiefs on the Plaza de Mayo in Buenos Aires.

Throughout the various Latin American countries, the majority of the military killers considered themselves "good Catholics." They did what they thought was "the right thing" for their country, a sort of perverse orthopraxis. In cases where some were plagued by a bad conscience, they were able to secure absolution in advance from a sympathetic priest.

During these years the superpowers of the world stood by watching on the sidelines and did nothing. They seemed content to let the Latin American oligarchies do the dirty work in the battle against communism. Under the presidency of Ronald Reagan the United States provided aid to these military dictators and Reagan gave them high praise, calling them "freedom fighters."

Once again these countries could not break the cycle of powerlessness, injustice, and violence. In the words of Enrique Dussel, once again the "Creole oligarchy took over the task of dominating people here" (Dussel, *History and Theology*, p. 100). Through such vicious "cleansing actions" any new political leadership that might have brought fundamental social change in Latin America would be completely wiped out for a long time to come.

VII
ROMA LOCUTA EST

"The trouble with Liberation Theology was that it was based on a view of man that is by far too optimistic." Nancy Bedford, Professor of Systematic Theology, in a panel discussion at I.S.E.D.E.T. on July 16, 1998.

Along with the deadly blow that was dealt by the political powers against Latin American Liberation Theology in the 1970's, an equally hard blow came from Rome. It was not bloody or violent, but it was devastating in its own quiet way. Latin America is overwhelmingly Roman Catholic. "Roma locuta est" or "Rome has spoken" carries enormous weight. No matter what is being said, it has the force of an absolute verdict.

On December 8, 1975, Pope Paul VI issued an encyclica which was to have great influence on the future orientation of theology. It was the tenth anniversary of the conclusion of the Second Vatican Council, and the Synod of Bishops had just held its third general assembly the year before. The subject of this papal epistle was a favorite theme of Paul VI. Entitled "Evangelii Nuntiandi," it dealt with the proclamation of the gospel or evangelization. In it the pontiff seeks to give an answer to three basic questions: 1) What power does the hidden energy of the Good News have in our days to shake up the conscience of man? 2) How far and with what means can this power of the Gospel transform humanity today? 3) What are the methods by which the Gospel must be proclaimed in order to be effective? ("Evangelii Nuntiandi," no. 4).

Paul VI makes it clear that he is aiming high. In his program of evangelization he wants to accomplish more than the conversion of individual souls to faith in Christ. The goal is rather a full transformation and renewal of humanity according to the promise in Revelation 21:5: "Behold, I make all things new" (no. 18). This means "not only to preach the Gospel in ever larger geographical areas and to ever more numerous populations, but with the power of the Gospel to reach and transform the criteria of judgment, the determining values, the points of interest, the lines of thought, the sources for inspiration and the models of life for humankind which are opposed to the Word of God and to the design of salvation" (no. 19).

This program of evangelization is as generous and as far reaching as the transformation of society envisioned by the Bishops' Conference in Medellín in 1968. While the Gospel itself is completely independent from any culture, the ultimate goal is for the Gospel and evangelization to "impregnate all cultures without submitting to any of them" (no. 20).

Now, however, Pope Paul VI leaves no doubt that a transformation of society must come from within. There will not be a new humanity unless first there are new human beings who reflect the newness of baptism and life according to the Gospel. "Only through the divine power of the preached message does the Church seek to convert both the personal and collective conscience of people at the same time as well as the actions in which they are engaged, their concrete life and environment" (no. 18).

Paul VI is fully aware of the desperate struggle with which whole populations particularly in Third World countries try to survive. He knows how they have to exert all their energy in order to overcome the obstacles that condemn them to live a marginal existence: "hunger, chronic diseases, illiteracy, exhaustion, injustice in international relations and especially in the commercial exchanges, situations of economic and cultural neo-colonialism which at times is as cruel as the political one, etc." He recognizes that the Church has the obligation

> to announce the liberation of millions of human beings among whom there are many of her own children: the obligation to help in the birth of such a liberation, to give witness to it and to insure that it be total (no. 30).

It is impossible to separate the work of evangelization from human development and liberation, just as the love of one's neighbor makes it impossible to preach the Gospel while "ignoring the extremely serious problems of justice, liberation, development and peace in the world" (no. 31).

The pope does not see the same sharp contradiction between "liberation" and "development" that the liberation theologians so passionately defend. Liberty, justice, human promotion, development, and peace are mixed together into one lump of dough. But while this encyclica does not contradict the message Paul VI had delivered to the Latin American bishops in the Cathedral of Bogotá when he opened their CELAM conference in 1968, he now draws clear limits to the type of social transformation he is ready to tolerate. One hears the stern warning in his voice and sees his right index finger raised when reading the Holy Father's admonition:

> There are many Christians who are generous and sensitive to the dramatic questions which the problem of liberation carries with itself and to the desire to engage the Church in the effort of liberation. But frequently they have felt the temptation to reduce her mission to the dimensions of a purely temporal project; to reduce her objectives to an anthropological perspective: the salvation for which she is messenger and sacrament, simply to a material well-being; her activity—while forgetting every spiritual and religious concern—merely to initiatives of the political or social order (no. 32).

With great passion the pope outlines the authentic liberation which comes from the Gospel, as announced and put into practice by his program of evangelization. This is a liberation

> which cannot be reduced to the simple and narrow economic, political, social or cultural dimension, but which shall embrace the whole man in all his dimensions including his openness to the Absolute which is God;—which therefore is joined to a certain concept of man, to an anthropology which can never be sacrificed to the demands of whatever strategy, praxis, or short-lived success (no. 33).

There can be no doubt that this encyclica is an outstanding and carefully nuanced teaching instrument. But then we have to ask: Who are those "generous Christians" who are reined in here by Paul VI? Who are the ones carried so far by their sensitivity to the dramatic aspects of liberation that they reduce the mission of the Church to the dimensions of a purely temporal project? Who are the Christians who sacrifice the spiritual and religious dimension of the Church blindly to the political and social demands of the hour?

We do not have to go very far for an answer. It is obvious that his stern warning is directed to liberation theologians. They are the ones who must be brought into line, in the pope's opinion. But not many of them in fact abandoned the transcendental dimension of the Church's mission. Not a single one of them would willingly give up his ordination for membership in a political party or trade the consecrated host for a party card. Rather, the liberation theologians seek to find the presence of God also in the political arena. They attempt to discover the sacred in the profane, the transcendental in the immanent, the spiritual in the temporal, the religious in the cultural, the eternal in the historical, the infinite in the finite, *finitum capax infiniti.*

Most of the liberation theologians do not equate these opposites. Rather, they see them in a dialectical relationship to each other and go back and forth between them. This is what makes their theological project so fascinating. But in this encyclica they are given clear notice that they must not go too far with their dialectical maneuvers and should not cross certain lines.

On the other hand, it must be recognized that there are some liberation theologians who upset the delicate balance. Instead of maintaining a careful dialectics they level important distinctions. When they confuse the temporal with the spiritual or the profane with the sacred, their theology loses its internal tension and goes flat. One example is Gustavo Gutiérrez's notion of a "single vocation to salvation" which surpasses all distinctions (Gutiérrez, *Theology*, p. 46). He pushes aside traditional "temporal-spiritual and profane-sacred antitheses" and the "natural-supernatural distinction" as obsolete dualisms (p. 43). In his understanding, the building of a just society by Christian and non-Christian alike "has already worth in terms of the Kingdom and the participation in the process of liberation is already a salvific work." Therefore Gutiérrez considers "the distinction of the planes a burnt-out model with nothing to say to the advances in theological thinking" (p. 46). This is not just a bit of theological arrogance. As we have seen in the previous chapter, it is also a notion that gave this Peruvian priest the wrong sense of history which ultimately failed him.

Juan Luis Segundo provides another example of doing away with the distinction of two separate spheres or levels. The way he sees it, "the Catholic Church officially abandoned the theology of the two planes and opened the way for a theology that was quite different: i.e. liberation theology" which is incompatible with the former theology. Segundo understands the declarations of the Second Vatican Council in this fashion, especially the Pastoral Constitution "Gaudium et Spes" (no. 22) which affirms that "all human beings are called to one and the same supernatural vocation and, thanks to the grace of God, possess the means needed to fulfill this vocation." He continues:

> As we have already noted, ecclesiastical authorities have continued to describe the function of the Church as a purely 'religious' one, finding support in other conciliar statements which clearly seem to set a 'supernatural' realm over against the realm of 'natural' human history. My point here is that the statements of Vatican II are clear enough to ensure that the basic theological foundations of liberation theology may not be declared heterodox" (Segundo, *Liberation of Theology*, pp. 141-42).

For the same reason Segundo has no use for Luther's doctrine of the two realms. Luther clearly distinguishes the Kingdom of God from all human kingdoms. For Segundo this teaching puts the eschatological work of God on too high a plane and man's action in history on too low a plane. While in his eyes the doctrine is a wholesome one because it relativizes and desacralizes every political power, at the same time it also relativizes and "deabsolutizes" [*desabsolutiza*] the hallowed claims of any historical revolution (p.144). This is the problem Segundo had with such European political theologies as those of Juergen Moltmann and his Brazilian disciple Rubem Alves (*A Theology of Human Hope*, 1969). For Segundo such a relativizing theology robs historical revolutions of vitality; its eschatology "seems to throw a dash of cold water on any such enthusiasm ... for new projects spawned by criticism and hope" (p. 145).

There can be no doubt that Luther would have cooled the revolutionary fervor of this Latin American with more than a dash of cold water. But in this case the cold water comes not from Wittenberg but from Rome. In "Evangelii Nuntiandi" Pope Paul VI rejects the interpretation of Vatican II made by Segundo and other liberation theologians and reaffirms the necessary distinction between the political sphere and the religious, the temporal and the spiritual.

In this encyclica Paul VI returns to a favorite theme. He picks up the subject of non-violence which he had announced already in his discourse of 1968 in Bogotá, when he opened the conference of Latin American bishops. Once again in 1975 he affirms that

> violence is neither Christian nor evangelical and violent or brusque changes of the structures will be deceiving, inefficient by themselves and certainly not in conformity with the dignity of the people.

He goes on to declare in even stronger terms:

> The Church cannot accept violence, above all the force of arms, nor the death of whoever it may be as a way of liberation ("Evangelii Nuntiandi," no. 37).

This is an eminently commendable stance. Who could possibly be opposed to the Christian principle of non-violence? But if this truth is so self-evident, why is it declared here? Above all, to whom is it directed? Beyond any question the recipients of this emphatic warning are the same advocates of liberation with whom many other sections of this document are so vitally concerned. It is the liberation theologians who more than others are expected to pay attention to it.

However, if we apply Segundo's principle of ideological suspicion to this papal exhortation, suddenly as with the twist of a kaleidoscope the entire color configuration changes. The pope's highly commendable stance turns into a highly questionable position. We have to ask: Why are those who seek human liberation warned so emphatically against violence? Why is not a single word said in judgment against those who use violence, torture, and wholesale slaughter in the defense of the status quo?

At the bishops' conference in Medellín in 1968 there was no reason yet to raise this issue in such a pronounced manner. At that time a general declaration of Christian non-violence was credible. But now seven years later, the situation is dramatically changed. When Paul VI sends out his papal epistle in December of 1975, the first waves of fascist terror have already been unleashed in Chile, Brazil, and Uruguay. The rest of Latin America would soon follow in the bloody and brutal suppression of serious social reform. The pope could not have foreseen the incredible bloodbath that was shortly to take place. Yet how could he rein in the potential violence of social reformers in such a one-sided manner, and not be equally concerned with the manifest violence of guardians of the old order? This pope was fully aware of the fact, after all, that prolonged poverty and hopelessness produce their own violent explosions.

In "Evangelii Nuntiandi" Paul VI does not fail to mention the grass roots communities. He recognizes the special value of these *comunidades de base* both as recipients and as agents of evangelization, especially in vast urban centers with their masses of people and anonymous life style. But he makes a clear distinction between the "ecclesial" grass roots communities and other base communities which have a critical spirit toward the "institutional" church.

It goes without saying that the pope is full of praise for the "ecclesial" small groups' loyal support of the church hierarchy, their avoidance of a "hypercritical" spirit, and their faithful adherence to the Magisterium of the Church. On the other hand, he points out the serious dangers of grass roots communities which do not merit the attribute "ecclesial"—the unstructured "charismatic" groups which find their inspiration only in the gospel. As such groups question and criticize the church hierarchy, they quickly turn into "ideological" base communities and become prisoners of a political option (no. 58).

Roma locuta est. Rome has spoken. With "Evangelii Nuntiandi" Paul VI took control over a theology which had tried to fulfill the hopes of millions of people by assisting them in a political and social liberation. Beyond any doubt he dealt a devastating blow to the Theology of Liberation, switching the track on which much of Latin American theology would travel in the future. In "Evangelii Nuntiandi" Paul VI rediscovered the inward-directed nature of the gospel, the personal strength which must change the individual human being before society can be transformed.

Something else happened in this document. The pope went beyond a concern for the individual person. He diverted the focus from radical change in the structure of society to gradual changes in cultural life as a result of the dynamic power of the gospel. Not revolution but change in culture would be the motto from now on. Culture was one of the most important and urgent elements in the mission of the church. But the question remained: Can the structural evils in society be effectively attacked this way?

The pontiff's new focus would heavily influence Roman Catholic church leaders. But it would also shape the thinking of non-Catholic theologians, as I was soon to discover.

VIII
A PREFERENTIAL OPTION FOR THE POOR

"Has not God chosen those who are poor in the world to be rich in faith and heirs of the kingdom which he has promised to those who love him?" James 2:5

The Third General Conference of Latin American Bishops was supposed to be held in 1978, ten years after the Medellín Conference. But it had to be postponed. Pope Paul VI died on August 6, 1978 and his successor John Paul I served only 34 days before he also died. Karol Wojtyla of Poland was elected on October 16, 1978 and began a long tenure as Pope John Paul II.

The Latin American bishops came together for the third general assembly (CELAM) in the Mexican city of Puebla de los Angeles from January 28 to February 13, 1979. The conference was inaugurated by Pope John Paul II. Although his personal presence had a strong influence on the deliberations of the church leaders, the third assembly had been convened by Paul VI and bore that pope's mark in many respects.

The stamp left by Paul VI becomes immediately clear when one looks at the general theme of the Puebla Conference. In Medellín in 1968 the bishops had assembled to deliberate on "The Church in the Present-Day Transformation of Latin America in the Light of the Council." Now in 1979, taking their cue from Paul VI's 1975 encyclica "Evangelii Nuntiandi," the bishops' theme in Puebla was "Evangelization in the Present and in the Future of Latin America." This is a significant change in emphasis. Their main goal was no longer the transformation of the continent with all its social, political, and cultural upheavals. Rather, they now focused on the evangelizing missionary task of the Church.

To use the bishops' own words, "Our mission of bringing God to the people and the people to God also implies building among them a society which is more brotherly" (*La Evangelización en el Presente y en el Futuro de América Latina,* Documento de Puebla, hereafter Puebla, no. 90). But one notes that there is a clear "first" and a clear "second." First comes the sacred mission of "bringing God to the people and the people to God." The building of a more brotherly society comes second.

For this reason Puebla was much more "Roman Catholic" in the traditional sense than was Medellín. It is mainly the bishops who are mandated to "bring God to the people and the people to God." While all Christians are needed in this evangelizing task, especially priests, it is the bishops upon whom the main responsibility rests.

Puebla bears the stamp of Paul VI in yet another respect. In his "Evangelii Nuntiandi" this pope had called for an "evangelization of the cultures," saying with great emphasis:

> What is important is to evangelize—not in a decorative manner as if with a superficial varnish, but in a vital manner, in depth and to their very roots—the culture and the cultures of man in the rich and ample sense which these terms have in "Gaudium et spes" always from the starting point of the person and always bearing in mind the relations of the persons between themselves and God ("Evangelii Nuntiandi," no. 20).

He does not fail to point out the unmistakable difference between the gospel and the various cultures. The gospel is independent from and superior to any culture. However, "the Gospel and evangelization are not necessarily incompatible with the cultures, but capable of impregnating all of them without being subject to any of them" (ibid).

This theme is now taken up by the Latin American bishops in Puebla. An entire section of their document (Puebla, nos. 385-443) is entitled "Evangelization of the Culture." But they run into a unique problem. After all, their continent has been historically Roman Catholic. In other words, it is already supposed to have been evangelized.

The bishops describe the original culture of Latin America as a racial and cultural mixture of the Spanish-Portuguese and the pre-Colombian Indian and Afro-American cultures. They maintain that in the sixteenth and seventeenth centuries the foundations were laid for a distinctive Latin American culture which was deeply evangelized so that its Catholic orientation became an integral part of it (Puebla, nos. 409, 412). "The [Catholic] faith came to be constitutive of its being and its identity granting it the spiritual unity which still lasts regardless of the later division in different nations" (no. 412). This culture is pregnant with faith, but often lacks the necessary instruction. Therefore there is still a need for further evangelization. It is a unique culture which finds its expression

> in a popular wisdom which determines the particular way our people live in relation to nature and to other people, in an understanding of work and of fiestas, of solidarity, of friendship and of kindred (no. 413).

The bishops point out the many manifestations of popular piety among their people: the veneration of the suffering and dead Christ, the devotion to the Sacred Heart, different forms of adoration of the Most Sacred Virgin Mary, the veneration of the saints and the dead, the processions, the novenaries, the fiestas for patron saints, the pilgrimages to different sanctuaries, etc. (no. 912).

This is the "Catholic" Latin America as loved by anyone who has lived in it for any length of time. Its culture is particularly "shaped by the heart and its intuition." It finds expression "not so much in the categories and the mental organization that are characteristic of the sciences as in the artistic form, in a piety which comes to life by living together in solidarity" (no. 414).

Since the eighteenth century, however, this culture has suffered the impact of a different culture, that is to say "the arrival of the urban-industrial civilization that is dominated by the physical-mathematical logic and the mentality of efficiency" (no. 415). This has created a massive proletariat and the control by the great powers which possess both the science and the technology. In this way the problems of dependence and poverty are increasingly made more acute (no. 417).

This is the other side of the coin. There is no doubt that the bishops at Puebla regard with deep suspicion the achievements of our urban-industrial civilization. It is a force which has brought serious ideological problems and "has come to threaten the very roots of our culture" (no. 418) by its foreign rationalism and its two dominant ideologies: liberal capitalism and Marxist collectivism. The Latin American bishops dislike one ideology as much as the other. While liberal capitalism practises "idolatry of wealth in its individual form," Marxist collectivism leads equally to an "idolatry of wealth in its collective form" (no. 542f). As far as these church leaders are concerned, both capitalism and Marxism lead not only to a defensible "secularization" and the legitimate autonomy of the temporal sphere, but also to "secularism," a view of the world which is completely immanent and man-centered and therefore can do very well without God (no. 434f). The atheism professed by the Marxists is paralleled by the pragmatic atheism that is lived out in the capitalist system.

The Latin American bishops at Puebla agree with Pope Paul VI in his rejection of these "new forms of atheism." They quote his condemnation in their own document:

> In union with this atheist secularism we are offered every day in the most diverse forms a civilization of consumption, hedonism raised to supreme importance, a will of power and of domination, and of discriminations of every kind ("Evangelii Nuntiandi," no. 55; cf. Puebla, no. 435).

These are the challenges which call for a new evangelization in Latin America. Implicit in this call is a demand to return to the original spiritual roots of the people which were so vital before the arrival of the urban-industrial age.

A particular warmth runs through the different sections of the Puebla document. The special spirit of this assembly is best expressed by the terms "communion" and "participation." In their "Message to the Populations of Latin America" the bishops declare:

> We believe in the power of the evangelical value of communion and participation to generate creativity and to promote pastoral experiences and new projects (Puebla, Message, no. 9).

The twin concepts "communion" and "participation" are the key terms which hold together the entire program of evangelization as it was developed by the bishops at this conference.

Puebla is generally best known for the provocative stance which the bishops call "the preferential option for the poor." It is a provocative stance because many people might bristle at this notion and ask with some indignation: "And what's wrong with being rich?" The bishops answer this objection in the following way:

> The pastoral opening of works and the preferential option for the poor are the most remarkable tendency of Latin American religious life. In fact, the religious [priests, monks, and nuns in religious orders] find themselves increasingly in marginal and difficult zones, in missions among the indigenous, in silent and humble work. This option does not assume the exclusion of anyone, but it is a preference of and a coming close (*acercamiento*) to the poor person (Puebla, no. 733).

It is in this spirit that the bishops affirm "the necessity of a conversion of the whole Church toward a preferential option for the poor with a view toward their complete liberation" (no. 1134).

The conference at Puebla was firmly grounded in the concrete reality of Latin America. The bishops draw a moving and realistic picture of the prevailing poverty on this continent. It is so compelling that it is worth our while to quote their description in its entirety:

> The situation of the generalized extreme poverty takes on, in real life, very concrete faces in which we must recognize the suffering features of Christ, the Lord who questions us and implores us:
>
> — faces of children who were beaten down by poverty even before they were born, by obstacles to their possibilities of self-realization because of irreparable mental and physical deficiencies; the children of our cities who are vagrant and often exploited, a result of poverty and the moral disintegration of the family;
>
> — faces of young people who are disoriented because they cannot find their place in society; frustrated, above all in rural and marginal urban zones, by the lack of opportunities of education and jobs;
>
> — faces of indigenous and frequently Afro-American people who live on the margin and in inhuman situations and can be considered the poorest among the poor;
>
> — faces of campesinos who as a social group live as if banished throughout most of our continent, often deprived of the land, in a situation of internal and external dependency, subject to systems of commercialization which exploit them;
>
> — faces of workers frequently badly paid and with great difficulties to organize themselves and defend their rights;
>
> — faces of underemployed and unemployed people who have been dismissed by the harsh demands of economic crises, and many and their families to cold economic calculations;

- faces of marginalized, huddled urban masses who are under the double impact of a lack of material goods while facing ostentatious displays of wealth by other social sectors;

- faces of old people, every day more numerous, who often are marginalized in a society of progress which can do without people who do not produce" (nos. 31-39).

As they describe their situation, the bishops in Puebla go back to many of the concepts expressed already in Medellín. About "institutionalized violence" they now have this to say:

> With deep pain we give witness to the fact that the situation of violence which can be called 'institutionalized' (both in a subversive and a repressive sense) has become worse, in which human dignity is trampled underfoot to the level of the most fundamental rights (no. 1259).

Faced with the inescapable reality of violence in Latin America, the bishops condemn in unmistakable terms the physical and psychological torture, the arrest and persecution of political dissidents or suspected individuals and the exclusion of people from public life by the government authorities because of their ideas (no. 531). But they hasten to add an equally strong condemnation of any form of violence by terrorists or guerrillas as an acceptable way of liberation (no. 532). In the prevailing political situation of that year, however, this seems a strange thing to do. All over Latin America in 1979, fascist dictatorships reigned with terror and violence. One wonders about the bishops' display of ideological evenhandedness. Was it meant as a face-saving measure toward the generals in their respective countries? Or was it merely an exercise in dogmatic correctness?

Yet the bishops at Puebla deserve praise for their unambiguous rejection of the so-called "Doctrine of National Security" in many of their countries. Although often justified as a doctrine that seeks to defend Western Christian civilization, it is more often than not "an absolute ideology which does not agree with a Christian view of man" (no. 549).

In describing the situation of dependency in which Latin America still finds itself, the Puebla document brings examples which could have been cited already in 1968 in Medellín. It points out that

> since the fifties and in spite of some successes, the great hopes of development have come to naught while the marginalization of large majorities and the exploitation of the poor have increased (no. 1260).

Emphatically the bishops push for urgently needed reforms:

> Nobody can deny the concentration of rural and urban managerial property in just a few hands which makes the demand for real land and urban reform absolutely necessary; this is also true for the concentration of power in the hands of civil and military technocracies that frustrate demands for participation and for the guarantees of a democratic state (no. 1263).

It has often been said that the Conference of Puebla continued and deepened the concepts which had been brought to light in Medellín. A typical comment is made by Germán Doig:

> With complete clarity one discovers both the continuity and the development of the themes of the authentic Medellín, a very important deepening of the channel which was opened by Río and Medellín. But at the same time a comparative look reveals a giant step forward" (Doig, *Diccionario Rio-Medellín-Puebla-Santo Domingo,* p. 12).

This is a very positive evaluation and high praise indeed. But while not everyone would agree with Doig, there can be no doubt that Puebla did present much more of a united front than Medellín had done. Puebla ended with one clear and unified document while Medellín merely produced a variety of committee reports that hung only loosely together. Yet these reports actually were a true reflection of the lack of coherence that too often characterizes Latin America.

In some important aspects, on the one hand, Puebla is indeed a faithful successor to Medellín. The bishops in 1979 clearly hear again the urgent call to repentance sounded first at Medellín and then taken up by liberation theologians. At Puebla they issue this call to repentance anew with their provocative stance of a preferential option for the poor. As in 1968, they deplore the economic dependence of their continent and the exploitation of the majority of their people. They are obviously moved by that strong sense of personal love which has always been a vital part of traditional Catholic piety.

On the other hand, however, in various aspects Puebla does not continue in the spirit of Medellín. To put it more precisely, Puebla does not follow the spirit of Medellín in the same way as that spirit is understood and interpreted by the majority of liberation theologians. In an obvious reference to Liberation Theology, the bishops in Puebla reject what they call "deviations and interpretations with which some detract from the spirit of Medellín" (Puebla, no. 1134).

The bishops' rejection of an allegedly false interpretation of Medellín is particularly clear in the treatment of grass roots communities. The Puebla document notes with great satisfaction that these base communities which had barely begun in 1968 have grown in number and vitality since then (no. 96). But now the bishops heed the stern warning of Paul VI, rejecting those *comunidades de base* which are "clearly manipulated by political interests and have separated themselves from their bishops" (no. 98; cf. no. 261). They are worried about those members of a community or even entire base communities which are influenced by purely lay institutions or have been ideologically radicalized and therefore have lost their authentic sense of being part of the church (no. 630).

Instead of being a "giant step forward" as claimed by Doig, Puebla is in this regard a giant step backward. An independent movement of lay people is no longer tolerated if they are not in close contact with their bishop. Such people become suspect as "ideological radicals." The door which Medellín cautiously opened has now slammed shut for independent grass roots communities. While it is true that the Latin American bishops deepen their pastoral concern for the poor in a most compelling manner, it is also true that in Puebla they seem more preoccupied with the issues of their own church than with the social problems of their abused continent.

When the bishops speak in Puebla about the challenges facing them on their continent at this time, their deliberations center first and foremost on the specific dangers they see for the institutional church. This may be normal and understandable. But is it enough? They obviously feel threatened by a "climate of greater liberty and a pronounced critical sense" which determines whether the Church's pronouncements will be accepted or rejected (no. 77). They are worried about the shortage of priests and religious workers who can no longer keep up with the population explosion (no. 78). They deplore the indifference which—more than atheism—dominates large sectors of intellectuals and professionals, young people and workers (no. 79). They are disturbed by the growth of religious "sects" and a "false interpretation of religious pluralism" (no. 80).

Everyone expects a bishop to attend to these matters. He should occupy himself with the acceptance of the Church's message, with the recruitment and care of priests and religious workers, with the mood of the general populace and the rise of new religious groups. This is what bishops do. The question here is one of balance. Those who have been shaped by the Protestant Reformation will ask whether the concerns of the Latin American bishops at Puebla went beyond the welfare of the institutional church. While the reformers of the sixteenth century—Luther, Zwingli, and Calvin—did not arbitrarily shatter the unity of the Church, they were willing to risk institutional unity for a larger, more demanding goal they called "the truth of the gospel." One might call it the liberation of the human race through the good news of Jesus Christ. This "gospel truth" was so overwhelming to the Protestant reformers that it overshadowed purely ecclesiastic affairs, often pushing them aside as inconsequential. But the Roman Catholic bishops had yet to arrive at a similar breakthrough.

A Protestant observer wonders whether such a strong concern for the institutional church is matched by a similar concern for the crying needs of the people the Church serves. If one compares Puebla with the declarations of the bishops at Medellín, one must conclude that in 1979 the Latin American Church turned back the clock of history. In Puebla the bishops moved with great caution, intent on preserving their turf, while in Medellín they had gone forward with a prophetic voice and a clear vision of their role in shaping a new society.

As we mentioned previously, Gustavo Gutiérrez has noted that despite the climate created by the Bogotá Eucharistic Congress, the bishops at Medellín realistically perceived the world in which the Church found itself and its place within that world (Gutiérrez, *Theology of Liberation*, p. 73). But in Puebla the church crawled back into this "climate that had been created by the Eucharistic Congress in Bogotá." Instead of embracing the harsh conflicts in the world "out there" as conveyor belts moving human history forward, at Puebla the Church snuggled back into the womblike warmth of its sacred halls.

Once again we apply Segundo's principle of ideological suspicion, remembering the bishops' moving description of the prevailing misery: In the faces of abandoned children, neglected elderly, disoriented youth, exploited campesinos and workers, marginalized Indians and Afro-Americans, one can recognize the features of the suffering Christ.

Yet that is not the end of the story. "Evangelii Nuntiandi" was written in 1975 at a time when military dictatorships were initiating their reigns of terror. When the bishops speak in 1979, nearly four years later, wholesale butchery is in full swing. There is no longer any doubt about who is the Roman governor crucifying Christ. Yet the bishops refuse to unmask the generals as the Pontius Pilates of their time. The prelates play it cool, keeping a neutral stance between the actual violence of the military and the potential violence of revolutionaries. In their refusal to denounce the butchers in their midst, the bishops resemble the Jerusalem temple hierarchy of Jesus' day. They proclaim God's "preferential option for the poor," but they close ranks and are silent against a hostile world. The window John XXIII opened, letting fresh air into the Second Vatican Council, was ever so subtly, yet firmly, closed again in Latin America.

IX
WHAT IS LEFT?

"The fall of the Berlin Wall changed everything. Those who talked so big before have now nothing to say." Ricardo Pietrantonio, Professor of New Testament, in a panel discussion at I.S.E.D.E.T. on July 16, 1998.

Liberation Theology in Latin America took three major hits. The first blow came in the second half of the 1970's when military dictatorships wiped out the revolutionary groups. With great violence and cruelty they put an effective stop to any radical transformation of Latin American society in their time. The second blow came from Rome. In clear, unmistakeable terms papal directives defined the boundaries of the social teachings in the Roman Catholic Church. The Church was to turn back from attempts at social engineering and resume her essential task of preaching the gospel.

The third blow came with the fall of the Berlin Wall in 1989. This cataclysmic event signaled the complete economic disintegration of most of the world's socialist countries. It was a great surprise to nearly everyone and a traumatic shock to more than a few people.

It should be pointed out with great emphasis that none of the Latin American liberation theologians looked upon the existing socialism in Eastern Europe—in German called *real existierender Sozialismus*—as a model for their own attempts to renew society. They had no love for any of these concrete expressions of dogmatic Marxism and were appalled by the rigid inflexibility found there. That being said, however, all of the Latin American liberation theologians were socialist in their basic outlook.

There can be no doubt that the very existence of socialist countries served as a kind of consolation for the liberationists in Latin America. Here at least was an alternative to the capitalist form of society which held sway everywhere else. Here at least one could escape from the iron grip of the "bottom line" mentality of profit and money-making that held the rest of humanity captive. As we have seen, it was in this sense that the bishops in Medellín made use of "the temptation of the Marxist system" as a counterpart to "the system of liberal capitalism" in order to declare their own independence (Medellín II, on Justice, no. 10). In their call to repentance, all Latin American liberation theologians aspired without reservation to some form of socialism with a human face (cf. Enrique Dussel, *History and Theology*, p. 134). When the Berlin Wall fell in 1989 with all the world-wide consequences, and enthusiasm for the socialist vision died, this hope lost its concrete expression and focus. There was now no real alternative to the all-powerful capitalist model.

IX

How would Latin American Liberation Theology absorb these three blows? Could it survive? If so, how much would be left? These and other questions prompted me to return to Argentina in July of 1998 to seek some answers. I was deeply grateful to former colleagues and new friends at the Instituto Superior Evangélico de Estudios Teológicos (I.S.E.D.E.T.) in Buenos Aires, where I formerly taught, for their help regarding these concerns of mine. Most significant was a panel discussion they convened on the present state of Liberation Theology. Following is a summary of the most significant contributions made on that occasion. I report these remarks faithfully in all their colorful detail and variety from my notes. They mirror the fascinating and often confusing reality that is Latin America.

I had prepared a short paper outlining my principal concerns; this was distributed beforehand to the participants. It quickly became apparent to me as our discussion began, however, that most had not read it. With all the polite friendliness that was shown to me, there was at first a stiff formality around the table. Pablo Andiñach, Professor for Old Testament and the Academic Dean, opened the exchange. Reserved in his initial comments, the Methodist theologian stated that Liberation Theology came out of a concrete historical reality. With the passage of time its emphases and perspectives had gone through significant changes. Many issues that were pressing thirty years earlier had in the meantime disappeared; other elements remained and in some cases had become stronger. This was particularly true for the healthy bible-study movement which had grown during the last ten years in Latin America. Now significant groups of lay people were studying the bible with great enthusiasm in their parishes as well as in the grass roots communities.

Next to speak was Willy Hansen, a fellow Lutheran and Professor for Systematic Theology. He also showed himself to be rather restrained. Continuing Andiñach's train of thought, he affirmed that Liberation Theology is a historical theology and with the changes in history had discovered new dimensions. But then he raised the question whether such a thing as a unified "Latin American horizon" (*horizonte*) or unified Latin American context actually exists. The real pressing problems, he maintained, today manifest themselves in different regions and do not concern the whole continent. "In this respect", he said, "we live in a new cultural era" (*una nueva época cultural*). As the ecumenical dimension in particular became important for the different faith communities, the churches must now also deal with new themes of personal identity, including the questions of differing local cultures and increasing globalization.

Pablo Andiñach interjected here the comment that the older, so-called "classical" Liberation Theology was always handicapped by a lock-step socialist ideology that cut off any serious dialogue with those who did not share this political conviction. He declared that a theology which genuinely seeks to liberate cannot espouse socialist views in such a dogmatic manner.

At that point my good friend and former colleague Ricardo Pietrantonio, a Lutheran Professor for New Testament, entered the debate. I always appreciated Ricardo's fiery temperament, and now he brought fresh life into the discussion. Observing how the whole situation had changed dramatically with the fall of the

Berlin Wall in 1989. he declared emphatically: "Those who talked so big before that event have nothing to say anymore."

Now José Míguez Bonino took the floor. A Methodist systematic theologian and the author's good friend for many years, although a Protestant Míguez had been among the first generation of liberation theologians—the "classical" veterans to whom Andiñach referred—and had authored several important books on the subject. He seemed bothered by the earlier remark of his younger colleague Hansen that there was no common perspective for Latin America. Hansen, it seemed, had internalized the message of Puebla about evangelizing local cultures just a bit too much for Míguez's taste and in the process had given up on an overall social connection that united the continent.

Míguez, a kind and peace-loving man, was trying to build a bridge between the contradictions. But I heard the mild reprimand in his tone as he observed: "Oh, no! In Buenos Aires, Mexico City, Lima, and elsewhere all Latins talk about the same problems—corruption in the police force, how to relate to our governments, frightening unemployment, urbanization, unhealthy concentration of the masses in the cities, and so on. It is well and good to work with local and indigenous cultures. But this does not solve anything. In the end our wonderful indigenous cultures get swallowed up by the massive urban centers where our native Indians lose their personal identity and cultural roots in the anonymity of our metropolises."

Upon hearing this harsh portrayal of the Latin American reality, Andiñach loosened his initial reserve. He described the current spiritual climate in Latin America in these depressing terms: "There is an enormous crisis of solidarity in all of our countries. Nobody has any confidence in the other. Deep distrust undermines the trade unions, political parties, health groups, and other organizations. This lack of mutual confidence runs much deeper and is more pessimistic today than was ever acknowledged by 'classical' Liberation Theology. The prevailing mood is that there is nothing we can build up together anymore."

Willy Hansen had swallowed the correction by Míguez Bonino without comment. But now he reentered the discussion. He remarked: "Today we have completely new themes of liberation to think about. We have moved on to other areas. We are concerned with women's liberation and sexual orientation and other problems of personal identity, for example. One theme that comes at us from all sides is the question of empowerment." It was interesting that although speaking in Spanish, Hansen used the English word "empowerment" for which there was apparently no Spanish equivalent.

For the first time Nancy Bedford, a Baptist and Professor of Systematic Theology, felt moved to speak. Agreeing with her Old Testament colleague Andiñach, she picked up on the pessimistic mood prevailing in Latin America that he had described. Her comment was that "classical" Liberation Theology had been far too optimistic in outlook. "It was determined by an anthropological optimism," she declared, "that was quite superficial and very shallow in its attempt to construct 'the new man' of socialism." I found myself nodding in agreement; Bedford was right.

Strengthened by this support, Andiñach again stated his criticism of the one-sided socialist orientation of "classical" Liberation Theology, adding the observation that it had consistently pushed aside the interests of the feminist movement as well as questions of different sexual options.

Ricardo Pietrantonio had become visibly agitated. He insisted: "Even if socialism came to an end with the fall of the Berlin Wall in 1989, the old, "classical" Liberation Theology addressed and denounced the structural evils which plague our society. This is what we urgently need today. Before that, my own Lutheran Church as well as the Catholic Church had never concerned themselves with the structures of society. They had always remained passive on a purely individualistic level."

Everyone seemed to be in complete agreement on this point. Pablo Andiñach emphasized again the contextual nature of Liberation Theology and then returned to his attack on the socialist outlook of its major early proponents. He described the research that was done in his own field of Old Testament studies in the United States by Marxist exegetes. He particularly chastized Norman Gottwald and other materialist interpreters of the Old Testament whose work found no acceptance whatsoever in Latin America.

Up to this point in the discussion I had not said anything. But I could not keep quiet any longer. Playing the devil's advocate, I referred to the encounter of Latin American and North American liberationists in Detroit in August 1975. I reminded the assembled professors of the tension that had existed there between a theology based on class warfare and a theology based on racial and cultural struggles. I challenged my Argentine friends: "Are you saying that you have given up class warfare? With your new emphasis on culture, gender, and self-awareness, have you taken up the agenda of the capitalist First World? Have you bought into Western cultural imperialism?"

My question seemed to irritate some of them, as was my intention. Systematic theologian Willy Hansen corrected me: "We no longer make such an absolute distinction between capitalism and socialism. We have overcome the tensions that appeared in Detroit. Class and race are not that far apart for us. They complement each other. They are different forms of oppression. Today they are intertwined one with the other."

Hansen received quick support from Nancy Bedford, his colleague in systematic theology: "For us as theologians," she insisted, "the main subject is God. We speak about that God who loves the weak, who loves the weakest more than others. Therefore we no longer talk about a Theology of the Third World. Here in Argentina we are part of both the Third World and the First World."

I asked the circle of professors how they dealt with the "classical" liberationists in their classrooms. They answered that they had the students read their works, but by and large these veteran Latin American theologians are treated as venerable figures of the past. "They are part of our history now," I was told. But the new generation of younger theologians recognizes the importance of these "classical" veterans and appreciates the vital impulses they gave to the church and her ministry.

With this observation our remarkable exchange came to an end. I was sure that if I traveled from Buenos Aires to any other center of theological reflection in Latin America—in Lima, Santiago, Sao Paulo, Mexico City or wherever—the story of Liberation Theology would be handled in the same way. While other theological faculties might add a few different facets and interesting nuances, the exchange would not be significantly different.

"Classical" Latin American Liberation Theology is not dead. But it is in the past, a part of history. Actually it would be more accurate and honest to say that it has been silenced for the time being. Always contextual, it has gone through many historical changes according to the context in which it was embedded. Or so the story goes.

But this view is at best only half true. A critical observer of the Latin American scene might even call it dishonest, a lie. In fact the pressing human problems out of which Latin American Liberation Theology came surging in the early seventies after Medellín have not gone away. The crying realities of poverty, hunger, institutionalized violence, corruption, unemployment, lack of housing, lack of adequate health coverage, lack of a good education, and many other needs have not been solved for the large masses in Latin America. In many cases these problems have become worse. Meanwhile, a crisis of confidence has emerged to the point that no one knows how far to trust the next person. The voices of concerned Christians should have become louder with the passage of time. But the opposite has happened.

In the wake of a "classical" Liberation Theology which has lost its vibrant voice, a deadly silence has spread across the continent. A spiritual vacuum filled with deep suspicion and distrust has grown. A lack of solidarity paralyzes people in their personal relations, in their political parties, in trade unions and other associations. The people have become infected with the defeatist notion that they can no longer build up anything together.

Several days after our round-table discussion at I.S.E.D.E.T. I had an enlightening conversation in Buenos Aires with Father Rafael Braun, a prominent conservative Roman Catholic theologian and Director of the Centro de Espiritualidad Santa María in the Palermo district. Father Braun said he never had much use for Liberation Theology; he had considered it intellectually bankrupt from the beginning. He repeated the same criticism I heard from the systematic theologians in I.S.E.D.E.T.—that the liberationists' concept of man was shallow and superficial and did not take the full force of sin seriously enough. It was an assessment I personally agreed with. And then, in line with Paul VI's encyclical "Evangelii Nuntiandi" as well as the message of Puebla, this brilliantly educated theologian told me: "What the masses of our poor people need and want are not some abstract theories about a more just, humane society. What our people need and what we in fact can give them is a concrete religion they can touch and feel. Such a religion finds its expression in saints they can venerate, in sanctuaries where they find refuge, and in personal pilgrimages in which they can physically participate."

As a Lutheran I had to disagree profoundly with the idea that we should increase the number of saints, sanctuaries, and religious pilgrimages. But I certainly could see the need for a concrete religion—"a religion one can touch and feel"—in Latin America today. However, new alternatives have come into being and other religious choices are now available.

Two weeks after these discussions, still in Buenos Aires, I heard a fascinating lecture on "The Challenge of New Religions" delivered by Walter Altmann, one of my former students who is teaching Systematic Theology in Sao Leopoldo, Brazil. Altmann described the growth of Pentecostal and Afro-Brazilian cults and communities which have spread like wildfire in recent years, particularly among the poorest of the poor in Latin America. Contrary to all predictions by social scientists and religious observers, "we are now experiencing literally an explosion of religious energy in the midst of a completely secular world," he explained. People are searching for something new which they cannot find in the established churches. Even the middle classes are being drawn more and more into this spiritual search. They turn to charismatic and spiritualistic rites in hopes of filling the empty space they find within. Instead of fighting this trend, the historic churches whether Roman Catholic or Protestant are well advised to ask what they can learn from this spiritual movement and how they can be enriched by it. (For a sociological study on the recent spread of Pentecostalism in Latin America see Jean-Pierre Bastian's article "The New Religious Map of Latin America: Causes and Social Effects" in *Cross Currents*, Fall 1998, pp. 330-346.)

Although its prophetic condemnations of the inhuman conditions in Latin America have died down in recent years, Liberation Theology is not dead. It continues on, but in a lower key, finding its expression in two areas. First of them is life in the grass roots communities. From their very beginning these small base groups of lay people were dedicated to a serious study of the bible, an enormous step for traditionally Roman Catholic Latin America where the bible was always a closed book for lay folks. For thirty years this movement became ever stronger until now there is hardly a diocese that does not offer courses in "*lectura popular de la biblia,*" bible study for the people.

As was true during the Protestant reformation of the church in the sixteenth century, the simple but serious reading of the bible can be a surprisingly strong tool for human liberation. These bible studies in Latin America today can no longer be completely controlled or manipulated by the priests or the local hierarchy. Lay members in these churches have become used to asking their own questions and are not easily silenced. At a regional meeting of lay delegates from different *comunidades de base* which I could attend on the outskirts of Buenos Aires, the participants decided that the time had come to begin a critical study of mandatory celibacy for priests on the basis of biblical testimony. Although the Vatican may resist dealing with this question, these Latin American lay people were determined not to let the matter rest unanswered.

The most vibrant expression of Liberation Theology to this day is found in love, in committed service to one's fellow human. It cannot be otherwise. As Gustavo Gutiérrez put it, "theology *follows*; it is the second step" (emphasis is Gutiérrez's). The foundation for everything, he insists, is "real charity, action, and commitment to the service of men" (*Theology,* p. 9). On this level, Liberation Theology in Latin America is not dead. In its quiet, almost inaudible way it still speaks louder than words.

Nowhere can this service of love be seen more clearly than in one of the sprawling *villas miseria* or fringe ghettos on the outskirts of a Latin American metropolis. When I visited one of these near Buenos Aires, I found a small self-contained city with 41,000 inhabitants. For the most part it had no real streets and no sidewalks; from their decrepit dwellings the people moved out along slushy and muddy roads. Here and there one saw a teenager sniffing glue from a paper bag. I was told that the police actually distribute and sell the real drugs. They do it in order to bolster their meager salaries. However, there was lately a strong rivalry between the federal and the state police that resulted in two rival gangs in the ghetto, bitterly fighting one another and occasionally killing a member of the other side. Throughout this small city the presence of drugs, weapons, alcoholism, and killing dominated everyday life.

These are the "cities" in which the forgotten people live, often subsisting by scouring the garbage dumps for food. They live in garbage; they live from garbage; and they themselves are considered garbage in a society that has no use for them. Since they neither produce anything nor can pay for anything as consumers, they are completely worthless to the rest of modern society. The best thing they can do is simply disappear. And yet they will not vanish or go away. If only there were not so many of them! They are a permanent disgrace. What is needed here is indeed a religion that one can touch and feel. But does that mean more statues of saints and pilgrimages to sanctuaries? Hardly!

Three Catholic nuns, Salesian Sisters, were living in this ghetto which I visited with my friend and former student Dr. Arturo Blatezky. It is called Itatí. The three women shared a small but immaculate house on one of the better streets. Until recently they had lived in one of the most depraved areas there. But they were assaulted and robbed several times by armed thugs, so their bishop ordered them to change their location. Although the Salesian Sisters are normally dedicated to taking care of abandoned children, in Itatí the three cared for 41,000 abandoned people. They held full-time day jobs as domestic help for rich families, and with this income supported themselves so they could live and work in Itatí. Although they taught some children, their principal goal was to maintain a spiritual presence in the ghetto. As we walked together down the muddy roads, they were greeted with much affection from all sides. There was no doubt that they generated an enormous amount of love.

We stopped at one corner and entered a simple chapel someone had donated to this forgotten city. Blatezky, a systematic theologian whose doctoral thesis on Liberation Theology *Sprache des Glaubens in Lateinamerika* was published in 1978 in Germany, pointed to a side altar. Above it hung pictures of Archbishop Oscar Romero of San Salvador and two other priests, all martyred for their committed service to the poor. The message was clear: These, not the holy men and women of a glorified past, are the saints of our present time. Gazing up at those pictures, my friend declared: "There! That is the real Liberation Theology as it is lived out in a praxis of love!"

X
WHY SHOULD WE CARE?

For just as the body is one and has many members, and all the members of the body, though many, are one body, so it is with Christ. For by one Spirit we were all baptized into one body—Jews or Greeks, slaves or free—and all were made to drink of one Spirit (1 Corinthians 12:12f).

Times change. History moves on. Once-revolutionary Latin American Liberation Theology has become "classic." Now the question arises: Why should we care?

In 1968 the spiritual climate throughout the world was one of great optimism. People everywhere were ready to make new starts. The biblical story of the exodus provided a fitting model for many endeavors and projects. Get up and get out of the land of slavery! was the theme expounded in countless sermons, lectures, and classes. "We shall overcome" and "Let my people go!" were enthusiastically sung at worship services and political rallies.

By the end of the last century this great wave of optimism ebbed, giving way to a mood of growing apprehension. Breathtaking advances in science and technology did not sustain a sense of confidence and assurance in most people. In fact, the opposite seemed to be the case. Now, years later, uncertainty still prevails everywhere across the globe.

Liberation Theology was a clear call to repentance. It sought to wake up Latin American Christians and recruit them into the urgent task of transforming their society. It always understood itself as a wake-up call, arousing people to a radical reshuffling of power structures that support unfair systems of benefits and privileges. This call to repentance was nothing less than a call to revolution, and its message resonated throughout the Christian world: The place of the church is at the side of those who are economically left behind. God shows a preferential option for the poor of this earth.

As we have seen, there were many reasons for revolutionary change in Latin America. The challenge of Liberation Theology came surging out of a real context of pressing problems. But in spite of the passage of time, this urgent context has not gone through a significant transformation. Thus Latin American Liberation Theology cannot be dead. Nor did it prove to be a "superficial thing or a passing fad" to use Juan Luis Segundo's phrase (Segundo, *Liberation*, p. 3). Its call to renewal is still as valid as it was in 1968, and its work has barely begun.

The liberationists' challenge to a profound new change of mind was directed first and foremost to the Roman Catholic Church, the most powerful religious institution in Latin America. In trying to convince his Latin American readers that a new world order had arrived and the old era of Christendom was over, Gustavo Gutiérrez explains the church's dilemma thus:

> Christendom is not primarily a mental construct. It is above all a fact, indeed the longest historical experience the Church has had. Hence the deep impact it has made on its life and thought.
> In the Christendom mentality, and in the point of view which prolongs it, temporal realities lack autonomy. They are not regarded by the Church as having an authentic existence. It therefore uses them for its own ends (Gutiérrez, *Theology*, p. 34).

Gutiérrez goes on to engage in a vigorous argument that the time has come for "an entirely worldly world" (pp. 34-38). But the Roman Catholic Church would have a hard time getting used to the new reality. As we previously observed, for Gutiérrez "the Latin American Church has lived and to a large extent continues to live as a ghetto church" (p. 58). The Church in Latin America has been unwilling to leave the historical cocoon that was hers since the Counter-Reformation and relinquish the traditional privileges she is accustomed to. But the ground has shifted under her feet.

In the last fifty years of the twentieth century Pentecostalism and other Spirit-filled movements swept like wildfire through Latin America. This phenomenon was not fully recognized in 1968 by the Bishops' Conference in Medellín, nor was it appreciated by the subsequent liberation theologians, although Christian Lalive d'Epinay published his book *Haven of the Masses: A study of the Pentecostal Movement in Chile* already in 1969. But it can no longer be overlooked.

The first Pentecostal churches came to Chile, Brazil, and Mexico at the beginning of the 20th century. Since then the movement has expanded to include the whole continent. It is present everywhere, from depressed rural areas with large numbers of indigenous people and migrant farm workers to the *villas miseria* on the outskirts of huge metropolitan centers where the poor congregate as the countryside can no longer support them. The movement made significant inroads into the middle class as well. Although it was initially downplayed as a foreign import mainly from the United States, current sociological research has abandoned this view. It now regards this religious presence as an authentic Latin American movement that must be seriously reckoned with by the Roman Catholic establishment.

French sociologist of religion Jean-Pierre Bastian in his thoroughgoing investigation of the Pentecostal phenomenon lists four factors which explain its appearance and surprising spread: 1) The process of globalization; 2) The urbanization of the campesinos; 3) The fiction of a democracy without any real foundation; and 4) The refusal of the Catholic hierarchy to relinquish its power (Bastian, "New Religious Map of Latin America," pp. 334-336).

With his observations Bastian gives an accurate picture of reality in Latin America. The development of modern means of communication has caused an unheard-of expansion of religious movements. As a result, Latin America is not only receptive to new religions such as Pentecostalism but also produces and exports new religious forms. The charismatic pastor/manager of a new sect now operates with the same unrestricted authority as was formerly exercised by the overlord of a hacienda or a patron in the countryside. The campesinos no longer live in distant rural areas but now form an uprooted proletariat on the outskirts of cities. Just like a former patron, the leader of a sect today offers structure and protection in the face of social chaos.

Along with his description of the religious landscape, Bastian draws a telling portrait of the Latin American political reality. After 1980 the continent experienced a new democratic transition. Military governments disappeared; elections were held everywhere. But genuine representative democracy did not emerge. The rule of the people has remained a fiction. Personal responsibility of individual citizens exists only as an illusion. Elections are corrupted by fraud, servitude, and destitution. They become "a ritual exercise that permits the settling of scores among the controlling elites under cover of electoral fever" (p. 335).

It is clear to the French sociologist that in this political context the Roman Catholic hierarchy has failed completely. In spite of a sense of renewal linked to Vatican II, the church leadership did not extricate itself from its complicity with the political elite so as not to jeopardize its own privileged position:

> The church thus continues to instrumentalize the religious demands of the masses through a corporate model of management in a nationalistic Catholicism whose mariological or christological devotions are its principal manifestation. ... Besides, in order to domesticate the rebellious wing of the clergy, whose pastoral practice is liberationist, the hierarchy has reinforced its policy of conciliating with governments, which are equally interested in demobilizing radical Catholic groups (p. 336).

We have to arrive at the same conclusion on the basis of our historical inquiry. Our reading of "Evangelii Nuntiandi" and the Puebla document brought identical results. In spite of some laudable positive efforts, it is clear that the Roman Catholic leaders have so far shown themselves incapable of making radical changes that are urgently needed. At the very least, we feel the following three steps are long overdue:

1. The church must leave behind once and for all a mindset that holds it captive in the Counter-Reformation, opening itself to enlightened solutions arising from the Protestant reformation. It should, for example, take a new, free look at lifting the ban on clergy marriage and the right of woman to be ordained.

2. The bishops should willingly relinquish their privileged positions of power and influence if they are serious about a call to solidarity with the poor. Instead of reining in rebellious priests and lay people they consider a threat to the hierarchical order, they should find a prophetic voice and demand justice for the many victims of military brutality in their lands, even if this requires an honest confession of sin for the complicity of church people in such crimes. Following the example of Archbishop Desmond Tutu in South Africa, the bishops can be of invaluable help to their people as they come to terms with the recent past and work together to heal deep societal wounds.

3. Since the promulgation of "Humanae Vitae" in 1968, any enlightened approach to the frightening population explosion in Latin America has been

blocked. Birth control remains a taboo subject in Catholic circles, along with other issues of sexuality and family life. The church must open its eyes to the pill as a fact of life and address the reality of the population explosion.

It is remarkable that although modern contraceptive aids were already available over the counter in pharmacies throughout Latin America, liberation theologians refused to touch the subject of the sexual revolution. While some of them were quite ready to ignore the pope's appeal to shun "atheistic Marxism" and "systematic revolution," they all backed off when it came to a control of the population bomb through artificial birth control.

In fairness, even the Protestants among Latin America's reformers toed the Holy Father's line on this matter and avoided the subject. Some radical voices among them even went so far as to welcome the misery produced by the population explosion as a catalyst that would hasten the oncoming socialist revolution.

The liberationists also directed their call for repentance to the entire world Christian community. In his *History and the Theology of Liberation,* Enrique Dussel captured the challenge in these words:

> The process of liberation itself is the only thing which will make it possible for the oppressor to undergo a real conversion. Hence only the underdeveloped nations of the world can enable the affluent nations to discover a new, more human model of human life and existence. Our role in the future is an interesting and important one (p. 146).

Christians in the First World have needed the testimony of their Latin American sisters and brothers in the faith to reveal the dark underbelly of unbridled capitalism, its merciless competition and ruthless exploitation when left unchecked. At the same time, Christians in the poorer countries must also apply this call to themselves, so that while they are preaching to others they themselves do not remain unconverted. After all, the "haves" in this world do not just live in developed nations, and the "have-nots" are not only to be found in underdeveloped nations.

We live in a world which has become very small. Because of cultural globalization and economic transnationalization we are all very much dependent upon each other. Dussel is right to demand a more human model of behavior on the part of the rich oppressors. But poor people can also worship crass materialism and neglect others' needs. The call to repentance is directed also to them; they too need a spiritual awakening.

William P. George remarked in his article "Toward a Common Morality" that "Catholic social teaching has been seeking a prophetic, creative and responsible middle way between collectivism and laissez-faire capitalism for more than a century" (p. 908). We saw this earlier in several declarations by the Latin American Catholic Bishops (Medellín II, no. 10 and Puebla, no. 542). After the collapse of Marxism, John Paul II added a serious warning against the spread of a radical capitalist ideology unwilling to confront the massive problems of marginalization and exploitation responsibly, content to leave solutions to "the free development of the market forces" in an irresponsible fashion ("Centesimus

Annus," no. 42).

To keep a watchful eye on the forces of the free market is precisely what should be expected of Christians living in Latin America. They are more exposed to the consequences of unchecked capitalism than believers living in industrialized societies. While Christians in the United States, for example, may be tempted to blame the poor and unemployed for their own misery, Christians in Latin America reject such cheap accusations. They have had first-hand experience with the ugly underbelly of unbridled economic exploitation; they have felt the cold indifference when the less fortunate perish. They know that disastrous human tragedy often accompanies the accumulation of great wealth.

Protestants in the North who equate faith with seeking one's fortune need to hear the testimony of Latin American Christians. German sociologist and political economist Max Weber made this same connection earlier when he wrote *The Protestant Ethic and the Spirit of Capitalism"* (1904-05; English translation 1930).

North American Protestants sometimes accuse the German churches of having failed in their social responsibility under the Nazi regime. German Lutherans were rightfully accused of closing their eyes and ears to the atrocities committed by Hitler and his thugs. The theological cause of this passivity and quietism has often been assigned to Luther's concept of the "two realms," and we shall deal with this in the final chapter. But it must be noted that similar accusations were also leveled at Roman Catholics who under the Italian and Spanish fascist dictatorships of Franco and Mussolini were equally blind and deaf to the voices of the tortured.

In coming to terms with the dominant political and economic ideologies of the twentieth century—communism, national socialism, and capitalism—too many Protestants have been, and still are, silent about the excesses of unfettered capitalism. While rightfully condemning the failure of Marxist economics, they have closed their eyes to the sins of their own economic system and their ears to the cries of those who are its victims. As long as our Christian faith does not extend to include the welfare of those whose lives are destroyed by unfair political, economic, or social policies, a theology of liberation based on the transforming gospel of Jesus Christ will continue to have an affective pull on all who suffer injustice.

Again we ask the question: Why should we care? Because Christians are bound to each other by faith. In our time the ecumenical movement has brought many fellow believers from a great variety of denominations and traditions together into a new unity as Jesus Christ's body in the world. One hopes that this cooperative pull of Christian forces will broaden to include all the world's religions in a spiritual configuration of caring that spans our new century and extends well into the new millennium.

XI
THE EXCLUDED

"You speak to us of Latin America. It is not important. Nothing important can come from the South. It is not the South that makes history." Henry Kissinger

This arrogant statement by the former United States Secretary of State has given rise to understandable indignation. One who feels outraged is Prof. John L. Kater, Jr. of the Episcopal Church Divinity School of the Pacific in Berkeley, California. The offensive quote appears in Kater's excellent summary of recent contributions of Latin American liberation theologians in *Anglican Theological Review* ("Whatever Happened to Liberation Theology?" pp. 735-773). Kater carried out his study at the Seminario Bíblico Latinoamericano in San José, Costa Rica. The reflections in this chapter regarding recent developments in Liberation Theology are largely based on his research, and the quotes in this chapter are taken from his summary.

The Episcopal theology professor counters the world-renowned statesman with a sharp protest: "Henry Kissinger was wrong. At least for Christians, the axis of the world passes among those who are its victims" (Kater, p. 772; Kissinger's statement is found on p. 769). But who is right and who is wrong? The jury is still out on this case. The statesman expresses an insufferable hubris and disdain. But one also hears in his words a hard-nosed realism and a warning against romantic enthusiasm. It is not without reason that Kissinger has been called a "Realpolitiker" in the manner of Bismarck.

There is one element of Latin American Liberation Theology that will outlive all outward changes. That is its discovery of the preferential option for the poor. To come back once more to an observation by Juan Luis Segundo, this discovery is not "a superficial and ephemeral fad." It is a notion that fills countless believers with courage and hope. Gustavo Gutiérrez, the father of "classic" Liberation Theology, still emphasizes in his more recent articles that the option for the poor is "the most important contribution of the life and reflection of the Latin American church" (Gutiérrez, "Renovar 'la opción por los pobres'," p. 269f—Kater, p. 748); for "poverty signifies death" (Gutiérrez, p.271—Kater, p. 738). Therefore "there is no commitment to the poor if we don't struggle against the causes of poverty" (Gutiérrez, p. 273—Kater, p. 749).

But what shape does this struggle against the causes of poverty take? What are the concrete forms of this determined commitment to the cause of the poor? The discussion is not yet over. In the meantime we know that it is no longer the poor who exist at the lowest level of society. As we have observed, there is a class of people even below them, the dregs of modern society that exist in suburbs, shanty towns, and ghettos. These are the "excluded" who live off garbage and are considered garbage. Most liberation theologians have come to the conclusion that "the primary reality for the majorities in Latin America goes beyond want and is better understood as exclusion: exclusion from the possibility of a decent life by social, cultural and economic forces" (Kater, p. 744). Hugo Assmann directs a cutting question to his sisters and brothers in Latin America: "Where is it found in the Bible that the poor, through their conscientious leaders or representatives, would be the drivers of a radical historical transformation?" He calls such claims an "ahistorical gnosis, a kind of terrorism of linearity, without true dialectic and without any attention to the principle of complexity that governs any true process" (Assmann, "Apuntes sobre el tema del sujeto," p. 126—Kater, p. 744).

It is obvious that the poor will not rise up as the great revolutionaries in the history of the world, much less will that happen through the "excluded." Even the revolutions of North America (1776), France (1789), and Russia (1917) did not follow such a clear, undialectical course. But how will the story go on?

The majority of Latin American liberationists have put a name to the culprit responsible for the reigning misery. They call it "neoliberalism." They have come to realize that political forces do not set the course; the vital decisions are made in the economic arena. No longer do political tyrants oppress humanity. Real slavery is carried out by economic bosses. This notion is, of course, vintage Marx. In a personal interview, Pablo Richard of the Ecumenical Department of Research in San José, Costa Rica told Kater in June 1999: "Hope does not pass through the taking of power which is both impossible and irrelevant in a globalized world" (Kater, p. 742).

"Neoliberalism" and "globalization" are two different names for the same reign of terror by an unscrupulous capitalism that can no longer be controlled by anyone. This period began with the end of the Cold War in 1989. While the fall of the Berlin Wall was a great victory for most of the "free world," for many liberation theologians it marked the beginning of a new chapter of ruthless domination. As there was no longer a counterbalance to the forces of capitalism, a "new world order" took over. The tone is now set by transnational corporations and financial institutions such as the World Bank and the International Monetary Fund.

In his "Liberation Ethics" Enrique Dussel describes the present point in history with these words:

> Modernity goes on towards its end, sowing on the earth, in the majority of humanity, fear hunger, disease and death ... among those excluded from the benefits of the World-system which is being globalized. ... It is raised as a criterion of truth, validity and possibility and destroys human life, treads on the dignity of millions of human beings, fails to recognize equality and much less affirms itself as responsible for the otherness of the excluded and accepts only the hypocritical juridical demand with regard to complying with the duty of paying a (fictitious) international debt of the poor nations on the periphery, although the debtor people perish. ... It is a massive assassination; it is the

beginning of a collective suicide (Dussel, "Ética de la liberación. En la edad de la globalización y la exclusión," p. 567f.—Kater, p. 748).

Already in 1995 Franz Hinkelammert of the Ecumenical Department of Research in San José, Costa Rica pointed out the irrational consequences of a seemingly rational system which destroys an enormous amount of human life. He observed: "The business oriented by calculating money and earnings rationalizes its proceedings, but this rationalization is the origin of an irrational process of destruction of the human being and nature" (Hinkelammert, "Una sociedad en la que todos quepan: De la impotencia de la omnipotencia," p. 5—Kater, p. 745). Hinkelammert's comment is completely in line with the biting criticism that Hugo Assmann issued already in 1994:

> Capital is the Giver of Life ... Do we perceive the novelty? What is new in the current world conjuncture is that capitalism has arrived at a stage at which it is presented as an integrated whole: market, liberal democracy and capitalist culture. It is the character of the integrated whole that it proposes itself to the world as a global solution. It no longer admits alternative systems and it is not disposed to make concessions" (Assmann, "Teología de la liberación: Mirando hacia el frente," p. 2f—Kater, p. 745).

Assmann's bitter complaint that the free market economy is now presented as the gospel bringing salvation to the whole world is affirmed also by Enrique Dussel who maintains that the neoliberal utopia of the total market, like that of Soviet Communism and Nazism, is a utopia "that justifies the existence of victims" (Dussel, *Ética,* p. 55—Kater, p. 746).

These are hard accusations. But the question is: How far are they justified? Capitalism has never claimed to be the salvation for all humanity. The author is not an expert in economics, and the arguments marshalled by these and other Latin Americans do not reveal a better grasp of that discipline. It is understandable that after a period of fascist military dictatorships the system of a free market with democratic elections may have appeared to some as a messianic miracle. But this has never been the view in the developed, industrialized democracies. In these societies capitalism has never been considered the savior of the people.

It is true that societies built on money claim their human victims. But where is a system that has not done this in one form or another? No social system so far could claim to be free of inequality. Hinkelammert's criticism should be directed not only at neoliberal society. Human reason is capable of only so much; then the rational morphs into the irrational, destroying human life and nature in the process.

Obviously these accusations are the complaints of disappointed socialists who find it difficult to give up former hopes. What might be more appropriate than bitter laments would be a frank admission of their mistakes and an attempt to sharpen their vision. A clear confession that Marxism has failed as a viable economic system is badly needed here. But for the moment nobody has come up with a better scapegoat than the free-market economy. There are certainly shortcomings in the globalization of markets which need to be addressed and fixed. But a sweeping indictment of neoliberalism is of no help to anyone. Condemning the World Bank and International Monetary Fund as the archenemy brings no tangible result. Calling capital the original sin feeds not one hungry mouth.

The historian Arturo Piedra struggles desperately and honestly with the question of how to confront the monster:

> We still don't understand how, theologically speaking, we can define or explain this big monster neo-liberalism. In the past we used to say, 'Organize a guerilla movement. Organize the unionists. Organize a popular movement.'
> ... We've had guerilla movements, we've organized unions, we've had popular movements, and we still couldn't defeat capitalism. In the 1980s we had an elaborate and sophisticated theory. Now we just say, 'We don't know.' It's such an invisible animal we now have it in our houses. So how do we confront it? (Piedra, quoted in Alexa Smith, "Latin American Christians Reshape Liberation Theology,"—Kater, p. 742).

Those who suffer the most from a clear assessment of reality are the poor and the excluded. They are the ones who always get hurt. It is true that most Latin American countries are burdened with colossal foreign debts that choke the life out of them. But even if the debts are wiped out, there still remains a host of tough problems which need to be answered. How did this indebtedness happen in the first place, and how can it be avoided in the future? These questions are more than just a "hypocritical juridical demand" as Dussel calls it. They require hard-nosed, realistic answers.

When the Argentine economy went into total collapse in December 2001 after politicians transferred millions into private accounts overseas, angry mobs crowded the Plaza de Mayo in Buenos Aires, protesting currency reform with the shout: "*Pan y Trabajo! Ajuste al Carajo!*" *(*Give us bread and work! To hell with currency reform!) The people's wrath is understandable. Who would not foam with rage as one's lifetime earnings are stolen by irresponsible demagogues! But the organizers of this demonstration were equally irresponsible, seducing the people by making them believe there can be bread and work in today's world without a solid financial foundation.

Kater observes that some liberation theologians now wonder why they used Marxist analysis in the first place,—not just as an assessment of the present human condition, but also as an understanding of the gospel and the Christian faith. They begin to perceive that a more radical proclamation of the gospel is needed, one which is directed to each individual person. They have turned to a more intense spirituality. As a result, some of these Roman Catholic theologians have been moved to come home, back to the hierarchical shelter of their church and its magisterium:

> As liberationists have turned away from political activism and towards new explorations of spirituality and Scripture, they have also reexamined their conflicted relationship with institutional Church bodies, and in many cases

reestablished ties with authorities from whom they had been estranged (Kater, p. 746).

In today's world which has become small for everyone, it is not only the methods of production and commerce that connect people. The communications net, the exchange of scientific knowledge, rapid travel opportunities, a common treasure of culture, art, and entertainment and more have created a global village in which all people know each other better and can love and hate each other more intensely. This does not necessarily make life easier. Often it is the same story as in our old neighborhoods: The more one knew one's neighbors, the less one liked them. This side of human nature is unavoidable and can often create conflict. The same is true for the people of Latin America who no longer live in romantic—or miserable—isolation. In this author's opinion, they must learn how to communicate their concerns in a way that makes sense to others. This cannot be achieved through a blanket condemnation of the international credit institutions.

A new awareness of living in a global village will require from each member a high degree of personal responsibility. One cannot constantly blame others; one must be ready to assume burdens upon oneself. This personal challenge applies especially to Latin Americans as they face the problem of overpopulation, for example. A steady rise in poverty accompanies a rapid increase in overpopulation. Until now no liberation theologian, Roman Catholic or Protestant, dared to touch this explosive issue. But anyone with a clear mind has to ask the simple question: "How can you bring more children into the world than you can feed?" Until Latin American theologians are ready to address that problem, their protests against globalization will fall on deaf ears. Sooner or later they must take a clear position on this ethical dilemma by declaring themselves either for artificial birth control or in favor of the papal instructions in "Humanae Vitae."

On the other hand, the theologians of Latin America have not remained completely frozen in their positions of thirty years ago. They have explored paths which, at least for them, are new. In a discussion about the role of Liberation Theology in a time of globalization, a group of Brazilian theologians declared that while they are not willing to abandon this theological project, they must now open themselves to new directions in a "lengthening and deepening of its conceptual, methodological and thematic horizon" (W. Altmann, O. Bobsin, R. Zwetsch, "Perspectivas da Teologia da Libertacao: Impasses e Novos Rumbos," pp. 134f—Kater, p. 749).

Ironically, the Brazilians' new direction for Latin American theology is the inclusion of the interests of Blacks, women, and Indians, the point at which North American theology had already arrived in 1975. As we noted previously, when Black, Native American, and feminist theologians presented their concerns at the 1975 Detroit conference "Theology of the Americas" they were reprimanded by Latin Americans for their faulty "class analysis." For this reason I purposely provoked my Argentine friends in 1998 at our I.S.E.D.E.T. panel discussion by asking whether their new emphasis on culture, race, and gender issues meant they had abandoned the class struggle. In 1975 in Detroit the North Americans were not able to present the same unified stance as their southern colleagues took. Yet clearly their multifaceted themes were theologically relevant even then.

The liberation of homosexuals as a theological issue was not raised in 1975 in Detroit. Since then, however, controversies over the ordination of practicing lesbians and gay men and the blessing of same-sex unions have torn at the unity of several North American Protestant church bodies, and these conflicts are not over. In Latin America, by contrast, this explosive issue was not even mentioned by liberation theologians.

The protection of the environment is an important concern for many theologians in the industrialized countries of the north. In 1975 this issue had not yet captured public interest, although in Detroit it surfaced in a peripheral manner. In Latin America this concern has arisen but is not viewed in quite the same way, i.e. as an ecological problem. It is articulated rather as an urgent *cultural* need concerning "the land," *la tierra*. In Latin America *la tierra* is of crucial importance as an issue involving the equitable distribution of land. In this sense the bishops had demanded a thoroughgoing agrarian reform at their 1968 conference in Medellín. But the plan was never carried out, and since then the land situation has worsened.

In 1998 Roy H. May addressed the struggle for the earth anew, but this time through the perspective of globalization. He pointed out the massacre of landless peasants in northern Brazil, armed revolts of Indians in Mexico, assassination of native leaders and the massive occupation of banana plantations by peasants in Honduras, confrontations and forced removals of squatters from lands in Costa Rica, the formation of a national movement in Paraguay, and evictions in Chile, examples which illustrated "that 'the earth', far from being a theme from the past, is all too present" (May, "La tierra en tiempos de globalización," p. 21— Kater, p. 756).

Leonardo Boff, calling for "ecological justice," sees a close connection between interpersonal relations and our relationship to the environment. He terms it "social ecology":

> When we speak of Social Ecology we want to say that a minimum of ecological justice is necessary for social justice to exist. ... Nature is wounded with the same logic that the working class is wounded. Social justice must go hand in hand with ecological justice. In other words, we must respect the plants' biological cycle, respect the trees, respect the soil.

He raises the demand for a "cosmic democracy" in which "The stars are citizens, too, the sun and the moon live with us." There is no doubt in the mind of this Brazilian that the type of society which was organized under the hegemony of capital is "profoundly aggressive and causes the breakdown of the ecosystems" (Boff, "Las tendencias de la ecología," p.7—Kater, p. 757). The serious damage that was done to the environment by the socialist societies in Eastern Europe, however, is simply ignored by Boff.

While all the Latin American liberation theologians are convinced that globalization is Enemy Number One, some realize that there is no escaping this evil. Pablo Richard of the Ecumenical Department of Research in San José, Costa Rica, clearly admits: "It is not about fleeing or marginalizing yourself from globalization, but living within it with a different spirit" (Richard, "Subjectividad, espiritualidad y esperanza. Algunas perspectivas para definir el sujeto," p. 30—Kater, p. 765). He defines his perspective later in these words:

> It is nearly impossible for the moment to construct an economic and political alternative to the present system of globalization, yet it is already possible to question radically its logic, its rationality, its idolatrous spirit. ... There is still no alternative to the system, but there is an alternative to the spirit of the system (Pablo Richard, "Teología de la solidaridad en el contexto actual de economia neoliberal de libre mercado," Richard, p. 8—Kater, p. 766).

Resistance to the spirit of capitalism is what is needed. But what is the concrete form of this struggle? There are already hopeful beginnings. Richard lists some of them in a personal interview with Kater: Efforts at land-friendly farming that protects the traditional peasant; alternative medicine; projects supporting Blacks, native peoples, women, and youth in gaining control of their lives (Kater, p. 766). These may seem like small steps which are insignificant in the grand scheme of things. But Sister Ana Francisca López of Venezuela comments that they can have revolutionary power. She compares them to small ants who devour giant trees to feed from the fungus they create in them: "So the house of power can be destroyed!" (p. 768).

Such examples testify to the resilience which a living faith in Christ has kept alive. The Latin Americans through the centuries have been held down by overpowering forces and still suffer from them. As Kater eloquently states, they are "shaped by the reality of a crucified continent and the biblical witness of the God of life" (p. 769). But the same can be said about the true church in all places and at all times. The "communion of saints" has always lived in conflict with the world surrounding it. Whenever the church of Christ is true to her mission, she creates an alternative community which can provoke opposition in the surrounding society because she promotes values different from the common norm. The living church is constantly engaged in a struggle with the cultures in which she exists.

For Roman Catholic Christians in Latin America this is a new experience. Their church never had to struggle against society. To the contrary, the Church dominated society from the start. As the bishops in Puebla pointed out, Latin America has always been a "Catholic continent" in which "the catholic orientation" defines the identity of its people (Puebla, nos. 409, 412).

If one puts the harsh condemnation of capitalism under the microscope of historical analysis, one finds that it is not a new complaint. The liberation theologians have warmed up a new version of the rejection of an "urban-industrial civilization" from which the Latin American Church has historically tried to distance itself. In Puebla the bishops complained about the threat to "the roots of their culture" by the "mentality of efficiency" and a "physical-mathematical logic" (ibid, no. 415).

At the root of this resistance lies an unwillingness to accept the spirit of the Enlightenment. Although Latin America's spiritual leaders would not hesitate to use the latest modern technological achievements, they close their minds to the driving spirit that produces them. They are still sitting inside the spiritual ghetto of the Counter-Reformation. With all the compassion one has for this "crucified continent" and its sorely afflicted Christians, one hopes they may catch a portion of the hard-nosed sense of reality expressed by Henry Kissinger. At this time of globalization, the hour has come for Latin Americans to catch up with the rest of the world.

On a visit to East Berlin in 1989, Michail Gorbachev warned his socialist comrades in the former German Democratic Republic: "Those who come too late will be punished by life" (Hans Modrow, *Die Perestroika*, p. 24). The same warning has to be directed to the leading minds of Latin America, especially those who are deeply disturbed about the plight of the poor. They must become committed to establishing the necessary vital links to the rest of humanity. Those who care about the future of the "excluded" must have a firm grip on their own reality, present and past. Catching up with the rest of the world's history will not happen without the enormous spiritual and intellectual effort needed to break out of the ghetto in which this continent has lived for far too long. The theology of Martin Luther, a theology Latin America has ignored for centuries, can be a great help in the task, as we shall see in the final chapter.

XII
FAITH THAT MOVES MOUNTAINS

For truly, I say to you, if you have faith as a grain of mustard, you will say to this mountain, 'Move from here to there', and it will move; and nothing will be impossible to you. Matthew 17:20.

1. Origin and Growth of the Pentecostals

On my visit to Argentina in 1998, whenever I left the commuter train terminal on the way to my host's house I would exit into the main street of Quilmes, a working-class Buenos Aires suburb famous for its soccer team and its beer. I always walked by an old refurbished movie theater spruced up with shining banners that proclaimed the joyful message: "New Life"! The building had been taken over by a Pentecostal group. On several occasions I saw large numbers of people streaming inside, not to see the latest movie but to attend the evening worship service. Quite a number of teenagers and young people were among them, many beaming with the superficial smile one often associates with "born-again" Christians.

I regret that I did not have enough time to attend one of their assemblies during my stay. But I vividly recall attending Pentecostal worship services with my students in the port district of Buenos Aires thirty years earlier. We did not sit on plush seats in a movie theater but on hard wooden benches in a simple shed with a dirt floor. Men and women were properly separated from one another; one could not be sure what might happen once the ecstasy took hold during worship. I clearly remember the climax: After an opening liturgy of songs, prayers, scripture readings, and personal testimonies, a growing chaos of loud shouts, shrill yells, heart-rending cries and whispered sighs assaulted our ears, a dome of cacophony beneath which the worshipers' bodies whipped back and forth in a wild, frenzied rapture.

Listening to the shouting of these poorly dressed, simple people all around me, I had felt enormous pressure to let myself go, to join in the bedlam, to yell out my own misery and pain. I had asked myself what was holding me back. The only answer I found was this: "Remember your proper German upbringing! One does not do such things!" Yet I saw how people left the church service visibly relieved. The emotional outbursts had clearly been liberating. At the time, perhaps to cover my own unease, I had merely commented to my students: "Well, if you can't afford a psychiatrist, come here!"

Now, as I walked past the former movie theater in Quilmes, I had to think of the important book by Christian Lalive d'Epinay mentioned earlier, *Haven of the Masses,* a description of the advance of the Pentecostal movement in Chile.

Lalive d"Epinay wrote this religious-sociological study in 1968 under the auspices of the World Council of Churches (it was published in 1969). I had read it with interest at that time and then put it aside. In those early years nobody thought that Pentecostalism would grow into the important pheno- menon it became for Latin America. Many who stopped short of calling it a movement of "crazies" nevertheless considered Pentecostalism one of those weird North American imports that could not take genuine root in Latin America. I, like many others, assumed it would never be on the same level as an indigenously grown Theology of Liberation. How wrong I was, and how easy it is to delude oneself! Since then, Pentecostal churches have sprung up like mushrooms all over Latin America. They are no longer strong only in Chile and Brazil, the countries where they gained their first foothold at the beginning of the twentieth century. Today they can be found everywhere.

Walter Hollenweger also came to mind. I had come to know and appreciate this engaging Pentecostal clergyman at the Bishops' Conference in Medellín in 1968. An ecumenical observer like myself, Hollenweger had given me moral support in my role as the secretary for the commission on Justice. More than once he had smiled at me reassuringly and made the sly comment: "Some of these ancient prelates must see in you the devil incarnate!"

Earlier, when describing the shifts in the religious landscape of Latin America and particularly the studies by Jean-Pierre Bastian, we could touch only briefly on Pentecostalism. Now we shall deal with this phenomenon more thoroughly.

The modern Pentecostal movement began in a small Pietist bible school in Topeka, Kansas. Charles Fox Parham, its director, had asked his seminarists to pray ardently for a new Pentecost in order to fill a cold and complacent church with new life. Then on January 1, 1901 at the beginning of a new century, the longed-for miracle happened. Agnes N. Ozman, one of the bible school students, experienced a "baptism with the Holy Spirit" and began speaking in an unintelligible, unknown language. She was "speaking in tongues." Glossolalia is an ancient phenomenon reaching back to the beginning of the Christian church. This ecstatic speech is often accompanied by spirit-filled dancing, the gift of prophecy, and miraculous healing.

The beginning of a new twentieth century had generated the customary gloom and doom of impending apocalypse; people hungered for the reassurance of salvation before the end came. As word of the student's miracle got around, a movement quickly spread out from Topeka into the Southwest. In 1906 a young Black Nazarene preacher named William J. Seymour was seized by it. After being excommunicated by his denomination, Seymour started his own congregation at 312 Azusa Street in Los Angeles, and this church became the center of a new Pentecostal movement.

The modern Pentecostals initially sought only to reform their own churches by freeing them from the empty faith of a soulless formalism. To a large degree they were products of the North American revival movement of the late nineteenth century and adhered to a biblical fundamentalism. But as they encountered increasing opposition from brothers and sisters in their faith communities, they left and founded their own churches, guided by a strong desire to be free from hierarchical church order and repressive administrative bureaucracy. Similarly they rejected strict dogmas and solid rules of faith. The freely moving Spirit of God must not be constricted in any way.

The rapid multiplication of Pentecostal congregations seems to be a miracle of its own. According to statistics by David B. Barrett and Todd M. Johnson, there were 3.7 million Pentecostals in 1900 worldwide. By 1970 this number had grown to 74.5 million, and by 1999 it reached about 450 million (Barrett, "Annual Statistical Table on Global Mission 1999," p. 24f). A large portion of this growth took place in Latin America. A movement opposed to any form of bureaucracy makes it difficult if not impossible to acquire accurate membership figures. But according to some estimates, ten to twenty percent of Brazil's population is active in Pentecostal assemblies. Today Brazil is thought to have the second largest Protestant presence in the world, after the United States. In Mexico Pentecostals are estimated to be the largest Protestant group.

Christians who strongly insist on personal freedom, as is true of Pentecostals, are prone to divide into subgroups. As a result there is a wide range of individual Pentecostal churches such as the Assemblies of God and the Church of God in Christ, to name only two of many. In addition to the older, long-established Pentecostal communities which still focus on the impending end of the world, there are now also Neopentecostal assemblies with a more radical outlook, and many of these are in Brazil. For them the kingdom of God is not of the future; it is already upon us here and now, in a very real and concrete sense.

2. Seized by an Incomprehensible Force

When the Pentecostals began missionarizing Latin America, the open-air service was one of their favorite vehicles. The evangelist would go into a town, at times accompanied by his wife, and gather together several interested people. The group positioned itself at a public place such as a market square, railroad terminal, bus stop, or busy intersection. Singing songs and playing guitars, banjos, or mandolins they would attract a crowd of hearers to whom they preached the gospel.

In his study of the Pentecostals in Chile, Lalive d'Epinay gives a vivid account of how these evangelization programs started out:

> It is no longer the priest—the man paid to speak about God—who talks to the people and transmits the message, but the cobbler, miner, seller of empanadas (meat or cheese fritters), in short the people one meets every day. He who speaks might be one of the passers-by, and the passer-by might well be a preacher one day. The Word of God is no longer the monopoly of specialists, to the great offense of the bourgeois and educated people, who are shocked not only by the language of the Pentecostalists but above all by their pretension in wanting to speak about God (Lalive, *Haven*, p. 46f).

With a sense of mild irony, Lalive emphasizes a distinct feature he observes, that this scandal for the middle class is actually a special attraction for the working class:

> What scandalizes the élite is just what touches the people. Even if the message is coloured with the dialect of Canaan or with slang, it is listened to because it is transmitted in the language of the farm labourer and the Chilean 'Cockney', by men who are living the experience they speak of, and live it in the midst of a social situation and in problems and difficulties which are shared by those to whom they are speaking. He who preaches is brother to him who listens, they belong to the same social class and share the weight of the same problems of making a living (ibid.).

This is not meant as a cheap way to sell oneself. It is an honest attempt to establish a sincere contact with the other. The newcomer is immediately welcomed as "brother" or "sister" and warmly accepted without question into the solidarity of a human community. Here he or she meets other people who have similar life stories: Family disagreements and splits, sickness, poverty, unemployment, obstacles on all sides. At the same time the newcomers witness actual miracles in this community: sick people get healed with God's help, others find the strength to cope with life. When they themselves experience a conversion and are "born again," they will be received as full members in the congregation of the faithful and share these benefits.

In the beginning the motto for the Pentecostals was "Chile for Christ." Full of enthusiasm they shouted: "We are out to conquer Chile!" Lalive reports a statement by one pastor: "When I first preached ten years ago, there were about five of us. Now there are thousands, and we shall go on growing" (ibid., p. 51). The Pentecostals are on a crusade. Conquest is their aim, and nothing less. Like other fundamentalists of the Christian or Muslim persuasion, they are determined to subject the whole world to the rule of their God. Obviously this is not an easy task. But in Latin America they have achieved a success which nobody would have thought possible.

Pentecostal worship services are no longer held in run-down sheds. Today former theaters, movie houses, dance halls, and other large spaces are taken over. One no longer sits on hard wooden benches but in plush seats. Pastors no longer wear a black suit, tie and hat as in former days. As Lalive explains, this was the dress of the first missionaries from North America (ibid., p. 78). Today one is more likely to see preachers in shirt sleeves. Mike in one hand, they stride up and down the stage gesticulating wildly with the other. Although they are still fond of open-air services, to the traditional beach and public-square processions have been added gigantic evangelization campaigns in football stadiums filled with 100,000 people. Many groups now have personal radio and television stations at their disposal.

It is all so fantastic! It seems like an incredible miracle. A thoroughgoing study of this amazing movement, published under the title *Pentecostalism and the Future of the Christian Churches,* was conducted by Richard Shaull and Waldo Cesar. Shaull, who died in 2002, was a professor at Princeton Theological Seminary and a Presbyterian. He was a long-time staunch advocate of Liberation Theology. Cesar is a Brazilian sociologist who at one time worked with Lalive d'Epinay in Chile. Both Shaull and Cesar were intimately familiar with the situation in Latin America. Along with a team of co-workers they followed the activities of Pentecostals in greater Rio de Janeiro for several weeks, analyzing particularly the life of a large Neopentecostal congregation called the Universal Church of the Reign of God (IURD).

The team unanimously agreed that the Pentecostals have had much greater success at gaining entry into the ghettos of the Latin American metro- polises than has been the case for the grass roots communities of the libera- tionists. They harbor no doubt that the poor of this subcontinent are represented more genuinely by the Pentecostals than by the adherents of Liberation Theology.

Both authors wonder how this has come about. In the first part of the study, Cesar attempts to explain this development from a sociological point of view. In the second part, Shaull searches for theological answers. Cesar repeatedly raises the question of the phenomenon's origin: "Alienation? Fanaticism? Naivete?" (Shaull/Cesar, *Pentecostalism*, pp. 22, 33). Shaull, the theologian, observes:

> In Latin America, the Christian base communities became the incarnation of this faith that created a new life in community among those dedicated to the struggle for liberation and that grew rapidly across the continent. Today the vitality and impact of these communities in society are much less evident, and they seem to have largely lost their former capacity to reproduce themselves (p. 210).

For Shaull, an important aspect of this is the simple fact that the poor could not care less about a rational analysis of "what was happening in the world around them, the social, economic, and political realities causing this destruction of life" (p. 160). The sociologist Cesar, on the other hand, is more vitally concerned with what the poor actually think about themselves (p. 22). This brings him to the observation

> that Pentecostals solve their relation with poverty better than the Catholics in the Christian base communities (CBC). The Pentecostals are less secularized For the CBCs, culture and religion are submitted to rational analysis and critique—which, according to the pastoral agents, can separate the truth from the dominant ideology. Thus the importance of popular education in the CBCs (p. 25).

To put it in a nutshell at the risk of oversimplification, one could paraphrase thus: The Pentecostals draw large crowds because they are less political and more spiritual than the Catholics with their Liberation Theology. While the *comunidades de base* put strong emphasis on education, political and human rights, emotion reigns supreme with the Pentecostals (p. 88).

The Shaull/Cesar study of Latin American Pentecostalism is lively because of its extensive use of personal testimony by participants in the Brazilian Universal Church of the Reign of God. In these personal interviews one gets a sense of the powerful impact this movement has on its people. Time and again one is amazed and must admit that a faith is at work here which literally moves mountains. A hope fills these people which transforms their often hopeless situations into a glorious victory of God (ibid, p. 22).

Simple women whose lives have been devastated by sickness, unemployment, and loss find the strength to gather their few possessions and make them available to others. They collect their scanty food supplies and bring them along with the gospel to others who share a similar fate. Juliana, a member of the Universal Church of the Reign of God, explains:

> We take the Word to others, we walked to many places, where no buses went. I had a place that was far away. Once we made a campaign for everybody to give anything, beans, rice, cookies meat. And they made those bags, those boxes that we could distribute in those places, ... we took food, clothing—and there was a lot of happiness ... It was like this, a comparison: I am here with you, right? Then they divide like this: I, you, and another person go on one street; another goes on another street, and another on another. And we hand out the things, we pray for the people, anointing people" (p. 20).

Rosa reports how her whole life was dramatically changed when she started attending the Universal Church of the Reign of God:

> After I entered the Universal everything changed. Even with my rigid boss it was possible to change. ... And also the doctor said that I would be never a mother. So I took part in a prayer chain at the church and by the seventh session I got pregnant (p. 33).

3. The Word Creating Miracles

The Word of God has a different meaning for the Pentecostals from the significance it carries in the Roman Catholic or the Protestant mainline churches. Like them, the Pentecostals also accept the bible as the written expression of God's revelation. Most adhere to some form of fundamentalism, believing in the verbal inspiration of each word of scripture. None would attempt to investigate the bible with the critical methods generally used by mainline Christians today.

However, the Word that creates miracles among the Pentecostals is the spoken Word, or as they prefer to call it, the Word in which the Holy Spirit is presently active. Their worship services are dominated by the spoken Word. A constant torrent of sounds, shouts and cries fills their assemblies. Cesar calls it "the exuberance of the word" and provides this description:

> The spoken, sung, cried, and murmured word. The pastor is not the only one who speaks. All can express themselves in some way: in hymns, hallelujahs, greeting of the brothers and sisters, testimony, strange tongues, and in choral response to the question shouted out on the speakers, after an affirmation of faith: 'Is it or isn't it so?' and the prolonged echo of the congregation: 'It is!' (Shaull/Cesar, *Pentecostalism*, p. 41f).

There is little variation in the central themes that are dealt with. Everyday problems of the people are the focus of worship services, repeated over and over without much change. But this is not a trifling matter. Here a constant daily struggle takes place against devastating forces which destroy lives. At the same time the victory of God over these sinister powers is celebrated.

The preachers are usually not trained theologians but simple women and men, ordinary people who from their own experience have an intimate knowledge of the demonic forces of alcoholism, poverty, drug addiction, sickness, and hopelessness. Therefore they are able to put the worshipers into a wild frenzy of rapture over the great miracle of delivery from these troubles through the Spirit of God.

The spoken word of proclamation expresses the constant fight against the devil. The sermon is not an exposition of a biblical text. It is a battle cry: "The Lord is the Savior! He is the Liberator!" (ibid., p. 47). The bible has become a launching pad from which one throws oneself into combat. There is no time left for a deliberate and detailed study of the holy scripture. Now everything is war, a fight against an overpowering foe, just as in a military campaign.

But victories can be celebrated along the way that also claim the whole person. Time and again one sees Satan being defeated and pushed back. Then the people break forth into a delirium of jubilation. Not all are capable of expressing their praise by speaking in tongues, but this is a goal they all aspire to. They are convinced that through this strange language caused by the Spirit they enter into the closest contact with God. As Cesar puts it, "'speaking in tongues' is the supreme moment of ecstasy for the majority of the participants" (p. 59). He also points out that a similar "wild happiness of being possessed by the gods" has been observed by Roger Bastide in the African religions of Brazil (p. 36).

It is not only through ecstatic praise that Pentecostals express gratitude for the deliverance they experience. They also make generous offerings from whatever possessions they have. Most of them do not own much, but they give lavishly nevertheless. While no one is forced to give a full tithe or ten percent, this is considered the biblical norm. Often the members are admonished to go further and to double and triple this percentage, even giving as much as fifty percent of their income. They receive a firm assurance that whatever one gives to God, he will repay in full measure. Bishop Macedo of the Universal Church of the Reign of God promises his believers that God even "has the 'obligation' to give an immediate answer to those who contribute" (p. 26). It is an attitude which Shaull characterizes in these words: "We give God what we have, and God is then obliged to give us what he has" (p. 154). Therefore it is not surprising that during the worship service people raise their purses or wallets toward heaven for a special blessing. Afterwards they still contain only the same few coins, but now they are filled with more than just money. "Now they also hold a hope, which allows the believer to even empty them in response to the appeals from the leader" (p. 36).

The purpose of the worship service is to motivate participants to put their entire life unconditionally under the reign of God. "From the moment of entering the church, everything is submission; but on the way out, it is mission" (p. 16). Mission means the sharing of God's blessings with others. Now one can no longer accept the world as it is, a good creation of God. Now the task is to conquer it for Christ's lordship and to subject it to the will of God. There is no room for halfhearted solutions or compromises.

4. Work of the Spirit?

The life of a Pentecostal is full of miracles. Some are assumed while others are real. But who can sort them out? The question at this point is whether all of these astonishing events are indeed creations of God's Holy Spirit. There are elements at work which undoubtedly are the result of one spirit or another. But is it the Spirit of God?

One wonders about the scandals, the revelations of fraud and swindle that appear in the press. The Universal Church of the Reign of God, which controls a huge amount of capital, has been accused time and again of using its vast wealth for the personal enrichment of its leading pastors. Mário Justino, a clergyman who left the church full of disappointment, maintains:

> Two things are essential in order to be a successful pastor in the Universal Church. The first is to have the capacity of channeling impressive offerings. The second quality is to know how to entertain people and hold on to them by their 'leashes'" (Shaull/Cesar, *Pentecostalism*, p. 27).

One's initial impression may be of a fraternal spirit that makes all Pentecostals equal with the same rights; after all, they reject any form of hierarchy. But in reality the leaders of a congregation possess unlimited spiritual power over their members. In his study of the Pentecostal movement in Chile, Lalive d'Epinay shows that their pastors have taken over the traditional role of the former plantation owner, the *patron*. In the rural setting of the past the poor lived as a huge family on a hacienda, protected and yet controlled by the *patron* who often turned out to be a tyrant. Today this function is carried on by a minister who for these believers is both a protecting father and a controlling leader with unlimited power from God (Lalive, *Haven*, p. 83).

The Pentecostals are a vital crowd, and being in their company is often great fun. But this can be misleading. There are limits to their openness in dealing with unconverted individuals. Shaull reports on the unsuccessful attempt by a member of his research team to explain her personal faith in Christ to a group of Pentecostal pastors. She ran into a wall of uncomprehension. Finally one of the pastors shot out the question most important to all of them: "Have you been baptized by the Holy Spirit?" This terminated the discussion. Since she did not possess the gift of glossolalia, she was hardly worth talking to (Cesar/Shaull, *Pentecostalism*, p. 196).

Not all Pentecostals show this kind of spiritual arrogance. In a Lutheran congregation in the United States, a couple who belonged to a charismatic prayer fellowship came to this author with a request to join our church. They described the exuberant joy which the gift of speaking in tongues had brought to their spiritual lives. I saw no problem in their becoming members of our community of faith so long as they did not consider themselves better believers than the rest of us. They insisted they did not have such a sense of superiority. Indeed, Martin and Ruth were soon among our most faithful, firm members.

Because of their astonishing growth it is not surprising that Pentecostals exercise an influence on the political power structures in Latin America, though this is not their declared intent. So far they are drawn to the most conservative political parties. During the Brazilian military regime most belonged to Arena, the party of the dictatorship. In Chile they supported General Pinochet and held commemorative services on the anniversary of the military coup which were attended by Pinochet himself. In Guatemala they helped General Rios Montt win election as head of state (ibid., p. 72). Their greatest political influence, however, comes from their support of ultra-conservative delegates to state and national legislative bodies (p. 25).

Political events are for the Pentecostals part of the gigantic and ongoing conflict between God and the devil. Such happenings are targeted by these believers in their crusades for Christ. Shaull recounts a typical comment by Janete:

> In terms of politics, the economy, I feel that our country cannot have too much hope. Brazil is a poor, badly administered country. There are no great hopes, especially when we consider the Word of God that each year we are approaching the end time (ibid., p. 22f).

Such shortcomings are a cause for deep concern even among those who are favorably disposed toward this form of Christianity. A number of things have apparently jumped off the track of reason and are headed for disaster, not only in the understanding of politics and economics but also in the basic comprehension of biblical truth. These worrisome tendencies cannot be blamed on the Holy Spirit.

Trained theologian that he is, Richard Shaull is aware of these defects. But he surprises us with his passionate defense of the main agenda of the Pentecostals in spite of their obvious errors. This Presbyterian professor hopes that the "wild" charismatics will shake up the mainline churches and arouse both Roman Catholics and Protestants from their complacency. Not completely without justification, he calls for a new discovery of Pentecost as the "founding event" of the Christian church, significant in the life of the earliest Christian communities (ibid., p. 138). The sad truth is that in most mainline theological textbooks the concept of the Holy Spirit is dealt with only in passing. In many Lutheran and other theologies it takes a back seat to lengthy discussions of the Word of God. A new recognition of the work of the Holy Spirit is sorely needed. With great emphasis Shaull declares: "The Holy Spirit is active now in the world ... and is changing daily lives, often dramatically" (p. 161).

Our mainline churches can learn from the Pentecostals a new appreciation of God's saving action in today's world. In Shaull's words, salvation of the believer is not only a progression from sin to forgiveness but also "from empty to full, from destroyed to prosperous, from depressed to happy, from anguish to peace, and from loneliness to life in the community of the church" (p. 146).

The fact that the Pentecostals were always talking about Jesus did not surprise Shaull He had expected that. But what did surprise him was "the way they spoke about Jesus: as Someone who was not only very real and close to them but who could be counted on to do amazing things in their day-to-day struggle for life" (ibid., p. 184).

A pastor of the Universal Church of the Reign of God advertises his church as the right community for postmodern people. Here, he is convinced, they will find what they are looking for:

> No subordination to large institutions; practical religiosity with emphasis on individuality; a break with certain values and principles patterned on a legalistic, bourgeois, and conservative ethic; openness to the new, the different and the unusual; abandonment of rigid and bureaucratic methods, and adherence to the simple, the clear, the objective and the direct, are some of the characteristics of the spirit of postmodernity (p. 13).

This has an attractive ring. Many of the features listed here can indeed be found among the Pentecostals. But there is also a dark side which is not mentioned in this commercial.

Shaull reports a question asked by the prominent Brazilian psychoanalyst Jurandir Freire Costa: "What does our public and private culture offer?" The psychoanalyst answers his own question: "Beer, football, and a trip to Miami. And what about the Universal Church? It offers a global perspective on life—a sign that our culture does not have only one rule of the game; it has several—and things that give meaning to life and death" (p. 30).

One cannot argue with this observation. On the other hand, the Pentecostal movement is a classic expression of that type of religiosity which was called the "opium of the people" by Karl Marx in his "Introduction to the Critique of Hegel's Philosophy of Right":

> Religion is the sigh of the oppressed creature, the heart of a heartless world, just as it is the spirit of a spiritless situation. It is the opium of the people (Karl Marx and Friedrich Engels, *Basic Writings on Politics and Philosophy*, ed. Lewis S. Feuer, New York: Anchor Books, 1959, pg. 263).

In his advocacy for the basic concerns of Pentecostals, Shaull also points out the spiritual search of a new generation of postmodern women and men who are no longer satisfied with the rationalist answers of the modern era (Shaull/Cesar, *Pentecostalism*, p. 170). It is true that a new generation is trying to break out of the tight corset of a strictly scientific worldview. It was Descartes, as Shaull correctly observes, who put them into this corset (p. 168). The guiding star in that experiment was a philosphical principle: "I think, therefore I am" *(Cogito, ergo sum)*. This was the foundation for modern science and all its achievements. But even in that age the philosophy of Descartes did not hold exclusive sway over humankind. The Church of Jesus Christ has also always lived the truth expressed by Anselm of Canterbury: "I believe so that I may understand" *(Credo, ut intelligam)*. In the postmodern period neither principle can be abandoned. Not even a new postmodern generation will be able to move forward without both of them.

XIII
RESPONSIBILITY—A PROTESTANT PERSPECTIVE

Your exile will be long; build houses and live in them, and plant gardens and eat their produce. Jeremiah 29:28.

1. Living In Exile

The majority of Latin Americans do not know what Martin Luther had to say about the reformation of the church, even though several expositions of Luther's theology are available in Spanish. One outstanding study explores the relationship between Luther and Latin American liberation theology. Walter Altmann, author of this excellent summary of Luther's principal positions, is a professor at the Lutheran seminary in Sao Leopoldo, Brazil. He points out the strong similarity between the German reformer of the sixteenth century and the reform-minded spirits within the Latin American church of today. "Would Latin American Liberation Theology be antagonistic to Luther's vision?" he asks. Then he concludes:

> It has often been thought so. And it is true that they have taken different paths, because their starting points are different. Taking into account their historical differences, however, they have similar objectives, not least of all in the matter under discussion here (Altmann, *Luther and Liberation—A Latin American Perspective*, p. 71).

Altmann is convinced that this is particularly true in the relationship between church and state under the rule of God. He is right with this observation. But he does not go far or deep enough. It is not sufficient to show that Latin American Liberation Theology and Luther are merely compatible. While this may give comfort to Lutherans in Latin America, a penetrating question needs to be asked: Does Luther have anything of importance to say to the Latin American liberationists? Can they learn from him?

Roman Catholic Latin Americans have always heard that Luther was a heretic who split the unity of the church because he wanted to break his priestly vows and get married. Thus they could safely ignore him. But many Latin American Protestants—Methodists, Episcopalians, Presbyterians, and Baptists, among others—although in the minority also consider Luther largely irrelevant to the task of constructing a meaningful social theory for our time.

This is understandable with regard to the average lay person. But it is surprising that none of Latin America's liberation theologians, including those who studied at German universities and had access to his writings, mention the Reformer's achievements—a failure that was bound to affect and even paralyze their efforts. By ignoring Luther theologically and historically, their passionate endeavor rested on perilously weak supports. It is an indication that they never progressed beyond the spirit of the Counter-Reformation but remained stuck in time at the Imperial Diet of Worms in 1521, where the young Emperor Charles V reportedly said of Luther: "This monk will never succeed in convincing me" (David I. Kertzer, *The Popes against the Jews,* p. 191).

The core of Luther's theology is the doctrine of justification by faith through the grace of God. This is more than a piece of abstract theology. Luther did not intend to split the church, nor did he want to start a new one. But it was vitally, crucially important to him that the church be held accountable. He loved his church with all his heart. Precisely for that reason he insisted that she be responsible for her ministry and teaching.

Responsibility means to give a response. For the church, taking responsibility means to respond by faith to God's grace and love given in and through Jesus Christ. Here responsibility means an accounting by the church for her actions and her doctrines. She must stand before the witness of the bible. Luther insisted passionately on the supremacy of the Word of God. He was prepared to defend with his life the principle that God's Word must rule the church, not the church rule God's Word.

This principle was of course unacceptable to the medieval church. During Luther's lifetime she fought against such an obligation, appealing to 1 Corinthians 2:15: "The spiritual man judges all things, but is himself to be judged by no one." Arrogating to herself this privilege of the "spiritual man," as The Church she felt no obligation to give an account to anyone. There were no limits to her freedom. She could act in a completely irresponsible manner, and in fact did so. Luther wanted to stop this arbitrariness for the sake of the church he loved. Thus he so strongly insisted that she be held accountable to the bible's written word.

Luther's new relationship between church and scripture became the foundation for a new sense of community. Just as the church must be held accountable for its action and speech, so also the individual must now be held responsible for his or her deeds. In Luther's concept the decisive judgment on individuals is passed not by church or secular court but by a God full of grace to whom each person must render account.

At the same time, the reformation freed forces that produced a complete secularization of society. Monasteries were dissolved and their possessions handed over to secular local communities. For the first time, clergy were subject to secular judges. The church was no longer unimpeachable and unassailable; ordinary citizens could now stand up against her. More changes were yet to come, many of them unforeseen and unintended by Luther. But a process had been unleashed that could not be contained. To this very day the Roman Catholic Church in general, and in Latin America in particular, struggles mightily against secularization. There are many reasons for her resistance, but it is a hopeless struggle. The course of the world will not be altered by her, nor is this the mission of the body of Christ. We are called to be the salt of the earth and the light of the world (Matthew 5:13f). The church does not have a mandate to dominate the world.

In countries shaped by the Protestant principle of scriptural truth, a new sense of personal responsibility produced fundamental shifts in the social fabric. This is one of the most significant legacies of the reformation. It is true that the Age of Enlightenment brought about a process of secularization, fostering new concepts of freedom not foreseen by the reformers. As faith was replaced by reason, many people no longer felt accountable to the Word of God nor thought they owed God anything. But in spite of this, it is also true that the Protestant awareness of individual responsibility still persisted with amazing vitality.

This element is painfully lacking in Roman Catholic Latin America. In spite of one's deep love for the people of this troubled continent, in spite of their genuine human warmth, their sympathy with the sufferings of others, generous hospitality and other virtues which one misses in other contexts—all qualities that define a catholic spirit—critically absent is a sense of individual personal responsibility. French sociologist Jean Pierre Bastian reached the same conclusion ("New Religious Map of Latin America," p. 335). Even if there are technically "free" elections, true democracy cannot take root in societies where personal responsibility among individual citizens remains an illusion.

The Protestant idea of personal accountability is a necessary ingredient of equal rights. Without this decisive element all attempts at true reform fail. Even a theology of liberation cannot change this fact. If this element is ignored, "preference for the poor" becomes that famous tranquilizer "opium for the people," temporarily numbing their pain.

Justification by faith, however, is by no means an anaesthesia. Its essential component is a dynamic relationship between two separate realms in constant interaction with each other: the realm of the spiritual and the realm of the secular. One may call these two realms by different names, but the important element is *the energetic tension between them.*

Luther does not leave any doubt that both realms—the secular powers of politics, economy, science, culture, and the arts, and the spiritual powers of worship, adoration, prayers, church organizations, and active service to one's neighbor—were created by God and are under his sovereign rule. But Luther saw a serious threat to their dialectical relationship. On the one hand, a church acting as God's deputy in this world controlled one's entire life and administered the work of the Holy Spirit through the sacraments. On the other hand, "heretical" liberation movements broke off all ties with the mighty church institution, often believing themselves so completely possessed by the divine Spirit that they no longer were subject to secular authority. To preserve a dynamic relationship between the secular and the spiritual aspects of life, Luther had to wage war on two fronts—against the absolute claims of the Roman Catholic Church on the one hand, and against the assertions of enthusiastic fanatics on the other.

In today's world, new confrontations have replaced the old ones. Not just one set of contradictions challenges us but a great variety of them. With the fall of the Berlin Wall the old antagonism between capitalism and Marxism also fell. But we are left with the contrast between rich and poor, between Third World and First World, between developed and underdeveloped, between the excluded and the elite, between the powerful and the voiceless, between the educated and the unskilled. The list goes on and on.

Simmering hostilities have continued between different faiths. In spite of secular forecasts pointing in the opposite direction, religion has not given up the ghost. We see massacres between Muslims and Christians, Hindus and Muslims, Muslims and Jews, giving rise to ethical problems and demands that we all must face for the good of our common planet.

At the time of the reformation the Roman Catholic Church had brought the work of the Holy Spirit pretty much to a standstill. By insisting that outside of her the Spirit did not function in the world, the Church for all practical purposes sent the Holy Spirit into retirement. Today many believe that the Spirit of God has nothing whatsoever to do with the existential functioning of this world. Life is determined in their opinion by uncontrolled economic forces with no connection to God and his Spirit. Having given up hope for any meaningful improvement on this earth, they no longer participate in the task of creating equitable living and working conditions for everyone but retreat into a cynical, single-minded pursuit of personal gain. They defuse the Spirit's energy by confining it to the private sphere of home, children, and an out-of-date church.

On the other hand, there are still revolutionaries possessed by one spirit or another who want to change the world without paying attention to the actual conditions that exist. Such reformers hope to usher in heaven on earth by forcing their idea of a perfect society on the rest of us. Some liberation theologians thought they had detected a legitimate divine call in these people. But in spite of all their passionate devotion, such revolutionary reformers have nothing in common with the Spirit of the living God.

Luther's teaching of the two realms is a challenge to all sides. It is anchored in the conviction that God rules over all people and the whole world. It confronts the arrogance of those who think they administer their sacraments or carry out their secular affairs without any influence from God's dynamic, living Spirit. But it also challenges those who claim possession of the independent Spirit of God for their own ends.

The exodus of Israel from Egypt is a biblical story which never loses its significance for the church. But it has lost the spark of immediacy that ignited people to action in the 1970's from numerous pulpits and lecterns. By contrast, the somber story of the exile seems to portray more accurately Christian existence in today's postmodern world. The Prophet Jeremiah's message to the exiled Israelites in Babylon in the sixth century B.C.E. finds a more receptive ear among many of our contemporaries now:

> Build houses and live in them; plant gardens and eat their produce. Take wives and have sons and daughters; take wives for your sons, and give your

daughters in marriage, that they may bear sons and daughters; multiply there, and do not decrease. *But seek the welfare of the city where I have sent you into exile, and pray to the Lord on its behalf, for in its welfare you will find your welfare* (Jeremiah 29:5-7—emphasis added).

We can be quite sure that the Jews at that time felt little enthusiasm for the welfare of Babylon, the land to which they were banished. But their own welfare depended upon this city, as the prophet told them. A great many Christians experience their life under capitalism in much the same way. Often it seems they can no longer tolerate the system, but their survival depends upon it. Yet capitalism does not remain forever unchanged. Jeremiah also predicted change for his exiled fellow Israelites in the near future: "When seventy years are completed for Babylon, I will visit you, and I will fulfill to you my promise and bring you back to this place" (Jeremiah 29:10).

As we previously noted, the Roman Catholic Church has never felt comfortable within a capitalist system. Her social teachings always maintained a careful distance from the spirit of capitalism. This can be seen in a long list of papal declarations such as the encyclicas "Rerum Novarum" by Leo XIII (1892), "Quadrogesimo Anno" by Pius XI (1931), "Mater et Magistra" and "Pacem in Terris" by John XXIII (1961 and 1963), "Populorum Progressio" by Paul VI and finally "Centesimus Annus" by John Paul II (1991). Because this church casts a wary eye on the excesses of the free market, it has often been labeled "outdated" or "out of style." But all serious Christians can share her basic outlook without rejecting capitalism outright. Luther's dialectic regards the free market or other economies with a critical eye, never fully comfortable within them.

2. The Two Realms

Luther's theology is tailor-made for life in exile. His doctrine of the two realms is designed to help Christians find their way in the exile which is this world. Economic systems and power structures change; emperors, kings, princes, and presidents come and go; feudalism, capitalism, fascism, communism and socialism take their turn. In all vicissitudes there is but one constant factor—the ultimate rule of God. For Luther, God exerts his governance in two distinct ways: through the "secular reign" and through the "spiritual reign"; in both cases his German word for reign is *Regiment.*

The Reformer is on this issue a son of the medieval church, which made a clear distinction between "spiritual sword" and "worldly sword." In the Middle Ages these "swords" were usually pointed against each other as the Church sought to maintain her supremacy of the "spiritual sword" over that of the secular authorities. Here Luther made a real breakthrough. While the two areas of God's creative work must be clearly separated, neither can get along without the other:

> For this reason one must carefully distinguish between these two governments. Both must be permitted to remain; the one to produce righteousness, the other to bring about external peace and prevent evil deeds. Neither one is sufficient in the world without the other (*Luther's Works*, "Temporal Authority," p. 92).

Actually this world should not have need of any political power structures whatsoever. Real Christians do not require temporal authorities or legislatures: "If all the world were composed of real Christians, that is, true believers, there would be no need for or benefits from prince, king, lord, sword, or law. They would serve no purpose" (ibid., p. 89). True believers have the Holy Spirit in their heart, "who both teaches and makes them to do injustice to no one, to love everyone, and to suffer injustice and even death willingly and cheerfully at the hands of anyone" (ibid.). But nobody is by nature a Christian or really good. Since we are "altogether sinful and wicked, God through the law puts them all under restraint so they dare not wilfully implement their wickedness in actual deeds" (p. 90).

There is always a dynamic tension between state and church. They are in a constant dialectical relationship with each other. It is in this soil that the personal responsibility of each individual Christian must grow. With great passion Luther explains how a Christian's responsibility is carried out in this world:

> Since a true Christian lives and labors on earth not for himself alone but for his neighbor, he does by the very nature of his spirit even what he himself has no need of, but is needful and useful to his neighbor. Because the sword is most beneficial and necessary for the whole world in order to preserve peace, punish sin, and restrain the wicked, the Christian submits most willingly to the rule of the sword, pays his taxes, honors those in authority, serves, helps, and does all he can to assist the governing authority that it may continue to function and be held in honor and fear Although he has no need of these things for himself—to him they are not essen- tial—nevertheless, he concerns himself about what is serviceable and of benefit to others (p. 94).

Where this personal responsibility of the individual is not a reality, even God cannot help the poor in their misery although he may otherwise give them preference in his own heart.

In order to put this view into action, it is absolutely crucial that individual believers be sent forth by their pastors and spiritual leaders into such personal responsibility. Thus Luther developed the priesthood of all baptized believers. Unfortunately, for the Roman Catholic Church this has been to the present day an impossible concept. She cannot accept the idea that her members may assume responsibility for their own lives, nor can she limit her own leadership to advice and consent, accompanying her followers with mere counsel. She has put all manner of laws on them, treating them like children on such matters as sexual ethics, planned parenthood, and family life.

Luther's view of Christian ethics is not a romantic illusion. Christians will always be a minority on our earth. Thus he provides a clear-eyed assessment of reality when he counsels in "Temporal Authority": "Do not be dissuaded by the multitude and common practice; for there are few Christians on earth—have no doubt about it—and God's word is something quite different from the common practice" (ibidl, p. 102).

3. The Sore Point

The particular relationship between political power and the spirit is a sore point in Liberation Theology. It has been an Achilles heel not only for Latin Americans but also for those liberating theologians among Blacks, women, and others who in their zeal to establish a heaven upon earth try to usher in the eschatological final destiny of all things. In their passionate partisanship and genuine personal commitment they tend to dissolve the necessary dynamics between temporal and spiritual authority, in the process destroying the dialectical tension between God's reign and political power structures.

This critique was raised as early as February 1970 by Lambert Schuurman, at that time teaching systematic theology in Buenos Aires. His comments were meant as a helpful Protestant correction for the new Latin American Liberation Theology. Schuurman, a member of the Reformed Church in Holland, urged his fellow theologians in Latin America to consider Luther's doctrine and warned them against a confusion of the two kingdoms. His advice, while ignored, was on the mark. It still deserves our attenton:

> I think what this wing of Latin American thinking needs is a demythologization of their concept of revolution. By doing so, they will probably be able to give more practical substance to their transforming plans. It should be evident that entering into the revolutionary act is a human decision and not a kind of mystical union with the incarnate God (Schuurman, "Some Observations on the Relevance of Luther's Theory of the Two Realms for the Theological Task in Latin America," p. 89).

In his debate with the enthusiasts (*Schwärmer*) of his time, Luther also warned: "You cannot run the world with the gospel." In other words, the rule of Christ does not yet extend to all people but only to those who believe in him. It is interesting that it was not a Lutheran but a Reformed theologian who gave this admonition to his contemporaries in Latin America.

Luther's dynamic of two realms requires Christians to realize their faith in concrete actions of service to fellow humans. This is the basis for the "priesthood of all believers." Political power structures have limits: "The temporal government has laws which extend no further than to life and property and external affairs on earth," he says. Christians observe these laws in their nation. But since the authority of the government has boundaries, the believer enjoys immeasurable personal freedom:

> For God cannot and will not permit anyone but himself to rule over the soul. Therefore, where the temporal authority presumes to prescribe laws for the soul, it encroaches upon God's government and only misleads souls and destroys them. We want to make this so clear that everyone will grasp it, and that our fine gentlemen, the princes and bishops, will see what fools they are when they seek to coerce people with their laws and commandments into believing this or that (*Luther's Works*, "Temporal Authority," p. 105).

The believer's freedom is a gift from God that implants within the person an awareness of accountability. The responsibility for what one is or is not to believe becomes an individual matter:

> Furthermore, every man runs his own risk in believing as he does, and he must see to it himself that he believes rightly. As nobody else can go to heaven or hell for me, so nobody else can believe or disbelieve for me; as nobody else can open or close heaven or hell to me, so nobody else can drive me to belief or unbelief (ibid., p. 108).

This new understanding of faith has far-reaching consequences for the way a Christian lives in society. The claim of unquestioned obedience and total commitment to a given system made time and again by totalitarian ideologies is a clear violation of the will of God and must be resisted by the Christian:

> How he believes or disbelieves is a matter for the conscience of each individual, and since this takes nothing away from the temporal authority the latter should be content to attend to its own affairs and let men believe this or that as they are able and willing, and constrain no one by force. For faith is a free act, to which no one can be forced. Indeed, it is a work of God in the spirit, not something which outward authority should compel or create. Hence arises the common saying, found also in Augustine, 'No one can or ought to be forced to believe' (ibid.)

In our discussion at I.S.E.D.E.T. in 1998, several agreed that Latin American Liberation Theology's view of human nature was too optimistic because it bought superficially into Marxist thought. While undeniably true, this is in sharp contrast to the view held by most Lutherans in Communist East Germany. A comparison holds some interesting insights. Shaped by Luther's concept of the two realms, Christians in the former German Democratic Republic managed to steer a careful course between full acceptance of socialism and complete rejection of it. Refusing to identify the church as socialist, its leaders identified it as a church existing within socialism (*Kirche im Sozialismus*). In contrast, by ignoring Luther's doctrine of the two kingdoms Latin American theologians, trying to be socialist at any price, missed the trend of human history.

Of course one could argue that because of its Marxist orientation, Latin American Liberation Theology had a certain sex appeal in the West. Many progressive or liberal theologians in Europe and North America—this writer included—felt some amount of envy. How boldly these Latin Americans could think, write and talk about radical revolution in their societies! Now this appeal is gone. George (Jorge) Pixley, a Baptist who taught Old Testament in Managua, Nicaragua, asked with some consternation: "What did the boom of Liberation Theology really leave behind for us?" (Pixley, "Qué nos dejó el BOOM de la Teología de la Liberación?," pp. 101-106).

How things have changed! My wife and I spent some time in newly unified Berlin immediately after *die Wende* (the turnaround) as the fall of the Wall is called in Germany. As we ate lunch one day at a diner in Potsdam, formerly part of the East, we observed a working-class family at a nearby table. While the mother and two teenagers were carrying on a lively conversation, the dejected father sat silently poking his fork at the food on his plate. Finally his wife glanced over at him and said in an exasperated tone: "O Dad, just get used to the market economy! (*Ach, Vati, gewöhn dich doch an die Marktwirtschaft!*)."

This disappointed and disillusioned father, no doubt a decent man, had obviously been a believer in the successful advance of socialism. But he overlooked one crucial thing: He had the wrong faith. Latin American Liberation Theology should have heeded the same admonition: "Oh, Dad, just get used to the market economy!"

Christians in East Germany and elsewhere under Communist rule showed the world how to live in exile. Luther's doctrine requires a similar attitude of Christians who live under capitalism. Like the Jews in Babylon, Christians build houses, plant gardens, marry, give children into marriage, sow and harvest. But they do not establish a "capitalist church." Their church will always be a "church in capitalism."

4. The Priesthood of All Believers

According to Luther, Christians in their different employments respond to a divine call. They have a specific vocation from God no matter what their labor is. They can say about themselves:

> Not only are we the freest of kings, we are also priests forever, which is far more excellent than being kings, for as priests we are worthy to appear before God to pray for others and to teach one another divine things (*Luther's Works*, "The Freedom of a Christian," p. 355).

In this wonderful freedom Christians serve and minister to their fellow humans. He writes:

> We conclude, therefore, that a Christian lives not in himself, but in Christ and in his neighbor. Otherwise he is not a Christian. He lives in Christ through faith, in his neighbor through love. By faith he is caught up beyond himself into God. By love he descends beneath himself into his neighbor. Yet he always remains in God and in his love (p. 371).

As he forged ahead with the reformation of the church, Luther opened a path between two extremes. On the one hand, there were those who had received a divine call—priests, monks, and nuns who accepted the religious life through vows of personal poverty, celibacy and obedience. Their vocation was recognized as the only valid divine call by the church at that time. Strictly speaking, Luther as an Augustinian friar was one of them. All other believers were in comparison second-class Christians.

While the so-called "religious" class was visible, concrete evidence of the kingdom of God, it was not considered part of the rest of the world. It is still the view of the Roman Catholic Church today that the "religious" are not responsible for making this world a better place. "Religious" means "other-worldly."

Diametrically opposed to the "religious" at that time were the enthusiasts, the *Schwärmer*. Empowered by the Holy Spirit, they felt a fervent personal call to turn this world into the kingdom of God where all would be holy and perfect.

Luther, by contrast, considered even the dirtiest and meanest of jobs to be tasks ordained by God and thus pleasing to him, insofar as they serve one's fellow human. The claim of the church's professional "religious" that they were following in the footsteps of Christ because they performed services similar to the ones the Lord had done was completely negated by Luther. The work of a marriage partner or a cobbler, tailor, peasant, prince, hangman, or policeman is just as significant, even though never done by Christ or the apostles. The only thing required is that Christ's people live under God's Word and Spirit. Only they are essential to Christ's kingdom. "It is by these that his people are ruled inwardly" (*Luther's Works*, "Temporal Authority," p. 100).

The freedom to love one's neighbor is a gift also to the poor and marginalized. They are no longer just parasites, welfare recipients, or human garbage. Through faith in Christ they too are called to be priests. In this role they also now appear before God, praying and caring for others. In this doctrine the true liberation of the excluded has its beginning.

A Canadian Roman Catholic theologian captures quite well the essential difference between Luther's approach and the Roman Catholic view. Gregory Baum, professor emeritus at McGill University in Montreal, describes two opposing concepts of Christian love that collide with each other. He devises a fascinating comparison between the East German "church in socialism" and Latin American Liberation Theology. The mainly Lutheran church population in the German Democratic Republic and the predominantly Catholic citizens of Latin America had a lot in common. Baum observes:

> Both of these theologies were contextual, both were action-oriented, both believed that faith had political implications, both expressed solidarity with the poor, and both affirmed 'the one reality' while believing in the glory of the life to come (Baum, *The Church for Others: Protestant Theology in Communist East Germany,* p. 143).

But there were significant differences between the two theologies as well. Baum pinpoints the main difference as a contrast between self-love and love for the other. His description is so lively that it is presented here in its entirety:

> The Protestant theologians in the GDR [German Democratic Republic] understood faith as discipleship, as being-for-others, as seeking justice and extending solidarity to the poor. Even though they lived in the GDR, a country of modest means, they saw themselves as belonging to the rich sector of the world, summoned by God to abandon their self-concern and turn to their neighbor, especially the poor and under-privileged. In this context, self-love or self-interest appeared to them as sinful.
>
> By contrast, for the poor in Latin America, faith meant believing that though the world rejected them, God in Christ has graciously accepted them. God stood with them, God enabled them to affirm themselves, to overcome passivity, self-doubt, and the false scruples induced by church preaching, and

to demand their place under the sun in the face of the wicked world that excluded them. The option for the poor was here an option for themselves. Conversion here meant abandoning self-contempt mediated to them by church and culture and receiving the new self-esteem mediated by the gospel. Thanks to Jesus, the poor were now able to love themselves and reach out for the material and spiritual goods they needed to escape from the structures that impeded them ... Sin was above all the return to the self-contempt and powerlessness they had experienced in the past (ibid.).

In these passages Baum gives an eloquent account of far-reaching differences separating the two theologies. Yet the contrast is not just between a "theology of the developed world" and a "theology of oppressed people" in the underdeveloped world as he claims. The difference cuts deeper. The message that you have to love yourself before you can love others has been preached in the First World by a wide range of voices, perhaps most forcefully by spokespeople for Black Power but also by leaders of the feminist revolution, gay liberation activists, and other proponents of one cause or another.

The freedom to express this opinion cannot be denied to anyone. But is a message of self-esteem and self-reliance the voice of the gospel? Where is the separation between propaganda and the good news of Jesus Christ? The gospel of Christ is a liberating force. It aims to free us from our many oppressions, including self-contempt and sense of powerlessness. But by focusing too narrowly on ourselves we lose the power of Christ as the true liberator. It is he who empowers people to overcome their love of self and to replace it with love for the other.

This is the heart of Luther's Christian proclamation. If it is abandoned for whatever praiseworthy motive, a different sort of inner logic takes over. Many Christians in Latin America have provided heroic examples of selfless love. Some of them even became martyrs in the process and gave their lives for the love of fellow humans. But a theological reflection that preaches self-love signals a wrong turn taken, an emphasis on only part of the message of God's grace in Christ Jesus and not even the central part at that. Even when all false scruples, passivity, and self-contempt are gone, the radical breakthrough has not happened—that which transforms the human being from a poor person into a rich one and a slave into a lord by replacing exclusive concern for oneself and one's people with care for the other, for strangers and those who are different.

According to Luther, all believers are priests by baptism. They perform their priestly ministry in the different vocations by which they earn their living. Although they may be a minority in the total population, through their labor they act as leaven in the dough. They are the "salt of the earth" and the "light of the world." They provide seasoning and enlightenment. But they do not dominate nor do they control.

This view is in sharp contrast to that expressed at the bishops' conference in Puebla: to preserve and defend the Roman Catholic culture in Latin America by maintaining a hierarchical structure (Puebla, nos. 409-413). It also clashes with the view of liberation theologians hoping to free Latin America by radical revolution—spiritually, politically, and economically. As much as they may differ on other points, neither bishops nor liberationists separate spiritual from political concerns. This kind of confusion provoked from Luther the following scathing comment:

> Now where temporal government or law alone prevails, there sheer hypocrisy is inevitable, even though the commandments be God's very own. ... On the other hand, where the spiritual government alone prevails over land and people, there wickedness is given free rein and the door is open for all manner of rascality, for the world as a whole cannot receive or comprehend it (*Luther's Works*, "Temporal Authority," p. 92).

5. The Ongoing Work of Creation

Luther's doctrine of creation is astonishingly dynamic. God has not finished the creative process. "God goes on creating," Dutch Reformed theologian Lambert Schuurman pointed out in 1970. Describing Luther's theory that "God is acting in the disguise of larvae" or behind different masks, Schuurman says:

> "Evidently Luther does not like the idea of a God who does all things himself, with the consequence of man's inertia. He firmly believes in God's activity, but it is never opposed to human responsibility" (Schuurman, "Some Observations," p. 88).

Again we point out that Luther's theology helped bring about an all-engulfing secularization process without clearly intending such a result. This is either to Luther's credit or it is his crime. He was firmly convinced that God continues to work among humans even when this process can no longer be controlled by the church. When he liberated individual conscience from external constraints, Luther in fact made possible a great variety of human responses to God's real presence in the world. As a result we now live with a great diversity of human achievements and products to be used according to the will of God for the benefit of our fellow humans. This plurality of divinely sanctioned gifts will not diminish but can only increase and intensify as we move into the future. We must assure that it does not turn into an unbearable burden or a curse. Everything depends upon that personal responsibility before God which humans are free either to accept or ignore.

Latin American Liberation Theology awakened the conscience of Christians around the world. Such an awakening was, and is, necessary. Juan Luis Segundo rightfully demanded, as we have noted, that this theological movement not be treated as "a superficial thing or a passing fad" (Segundo, *Liberation*, p. 3). It is a call to repentance, addressed not only to Latin Americans but to all who belong to the worldwide church of Jesus Christ. Its lasting contribution is the discovery of a special preference which the God of the bible has for the poor and excluded. No longer can wealthy Christians be content with their riches and ignore the misery of the economically oppressed and neglected. God will not tolerate the self-righteous assertion that the poor have only themselves to blame for their lot.

But by the same token, the poor are not free from accountability. They cannot abdicate personal responsibility with the excuse that there is nothing they can do to change their destiny.

The Protestant theology that arose out of the Reformation and nourished the Age of Enlightenment can be a helpful compass in this sorely needed liberation. But it cannot provide direction so long as the Roman Catholic Church refuses its believers the right to make basic decisions in their personal lives. As we have noted repeatedly, this is especially necessary in questions of sexual behavior, birth control, and family life. But a need for more personal responsibility reaches into communal life as well. A promising effort to raise individual awareness is made by the grass roots communities, where Christian lay people take personal initiative to shape a new life for their communities. The time has come for all of Latin America, with or without the blessing of the church, to take that last step to maturity.

In today's world it is not enough to be mere consumers of modern advances in technology, science, medicine, or economics. All societies and cultures must be able to take a creative part in the generation of such gifts. But this cannot happen without the help of a free and enterprising spirit. And that means a clear affirmation of the spiritual foundation that so influenced the awakening of the secular enlightenment.

In our age people have become increasingly aware that a much-touted "progress" will not fulfill their hopes and dreams. As the human race searches for new points of reference, some look backward to a more indigenous past. But the clock of history cannot not be turned back. Pat generalities such as a mindless railing against globalization will sink without a trace.

Living as exiles within free-market capitalism will continually challenge Christians. Luther's admonition means for us today a responsible churchmanship that is always vigilant in protecting the human dignity of all. In this spirit, Liberation Theology must be able to show the struggling peoples of Latin America and others in similar situations around the world how to assume individual responsibilities and commitments which may not have previously been allowed or demanded of them. Only through personal priesthood in the light of the Gospel can Liberation Theology lead people of faith to "leaven," "season," and give "light" to the world. Only thus can it once again make the message of St. Paul concrete: "If one member suffers, all suffer together" (1 Corinthians 12:26).

BIBLIOGRAPHY

REFERENCE WORKS
Doig, Germán. *Diccionario Río-Medellín-Puebla-Santo Domingo.* Bogotá: San Pablo, 1994.
Luther's Works. American Edition. Philadelphia: Muhlenberg Press. "The Freedom of a Christian, vol. 31, 1957; "Temporal Authority," vol. 45, 1962.
Medellín Documents:
———. "La Iglesia en la Actual Transformación en América Latina a la Luz del Concilio." Vol. I, Ponencias; vol. II, Conclusiones. Bogotá: Secretariado General del CELAM, 1968.
———. "The Church in the Present-Day Transformation of Latin America in the Light of the Council." Vol. I Position Papers [Medellín I]; vol. II Conclusions [Medellín II]. Bogotá: General Secretariat of CELAM, 1970.
Puebla Document: "La Evangelización en el Presente y en el Futuro de América Latina." Buenos Aires: Conferencia Episcopal Argentina, 1979.
Papal Encyclicals:
———. Pope Paul VI. "Evangelii Nuntiandi." 21st edition. Buenos Aires:Paulinas, 1998.
———. Pope John Paul II. "Centesimus Annus." Buenos Aires: Santillana S.A. de Ediciones, 1991.

GENERAL LITERATURE
Altmann, Walter. *Luther and Liberation: A Latin American Perspective.* Minneapolis: Fortress Press, 1992.
———. "Luther's Theology and Liberation Theology." In Lutherans in Brazil, 1990: History, Theology, Perspectives, edited by Gottfried Brakemeier and Walter Altmann, pp. 67-80. Sao Leopoldo: Post Graduate Institute of the IECLB, 1989.
———. "The Reception of Luther's Concept of Freedom in Latin America." In *Lutherjahrbuch 1995*, edited by Helmar Junghaus, 167-88.
Alves, Rubem A. *A Theology of Hope.* Washington D.C.:CorpusBooks, 1969.
———. "Is there any Future for Protestantism in Latin America?" In *Lutheran Quarterly,* February 1970, pp. 49-59.
Assmann, Hugo. *Theology for a Nomad Church.* Maryknoll, NY: Orbis Books, 1976.
———."Apuntes sobre el tema del sujeto." In *Perfiles teológicos para un nuevo milenio*, edited by J. Duque. San José, Costa Rica: DEJ, 1997.
———."Teología de la liberación: Mirando hacia el frente." In *PASOS* 55, 1994.

Bahmann, Manfred K. "Lutherans Plunge into the Third World." In *Lutheran Quarterly* 22/1 (Feb. 1970), pp. 4-10.
---. "Ideology and Faith in Latin America." In *Lutheran Quarterly* 23/2 (May 1971), pp. 107-24.
Barrett, David and Johnson, Todd. "Annual Statistical Table on Global Mission 1999." In *International Bulletin of Missionary Research* 23/1 (January 1999, pp. 24f.
Bastian, Jean-Pierre. "The New Religious Map of Latin America: Causes and Social Effects." In *Cross Currents,* fall 1998, pp. 330-345.
Baum, Gregory. *The Church for Others: Protestant Theology in Communist East Germany.* Grand Rapids: William Eerdmans, 1996.
Blatezky, Arturo. "Sprache des Glaubens in Lateinamerika." in *Studies in the Intercultural History of Christianity.* Frankfurt am Main: Peter Lang, 1978.
Boff, Leonardo, O.F.M. *Jesus Christ Liberator—A Critical Christology for Our Time.* Maryknoll, NY: Orbis Books, 1978.
---. "Luther, the Reformation, and Liberation." In *Faith Born in the Struggle for Life: A Reading of Protestant Faith in Latin America Today*, edited by Dow Kirkpatrick. Grand Rapids: William Eerdmans, 1988, pp. 195-212.
---. "Las tendencias de la ecología," in *PASOS 68,* 1996.
Bornkamm, Heinrich. *Luther's Doctrine of the Two Kingdoms in the Context of His Faith.* Philadelphia: Fortress Press, 1964.
Brakemeier, Gottfried. "Justification by Grace and Liberation Theology: A Comparison." In *Ecumenical Review* 40/2 (April 1988), pp. 215-22.
---. "Interpreting the Doctrine of the Two Kingdoms: God's Kingship in the Church and in Politics." In *Word and World* 7/1 (winter 1987), pp. 43-58.
Croatto, J.S., C.M. *Alianza y Experiencia Salvífica en la Biblia.* Buenos Aires: Ediciones Paulinas, 1964.
Diez-Alegría, José María. *I Believe in Hope.* Garden City, NY: 1974.
Donini, Antonio O. *Religion y Sociedad.* Buenos Aires: Editorial Docencia, 1985.
Dussel, Enrique. *History and the Theology of Liberation.* Maryknoll, NY: Orbis Books, 1976.
---. "Ética de la liberación. En la edad de la globalización y la exclusión." In *UAM-I* (1998). Mexico: UNAM.
Freire, Paulo. *Education For Critical Consciousness.* Continuum Book. New York: Seabury Press, 1973.
George, William P. "Toward a Common Morality." In *The Christian Century*, October. 7, 1998.
Goulet, Denis. *A New Moral Order—Development Ethics and Liberation Theology.* Maryknoll, NY: Orbis Books, 1974.
Gutiérrez, Gustavo. *A Theology of Liberation.* 15th anniv. ed. Maryknoll, NY: Orbis Books, 1988.
---. "Renovar 'la opción por los pobres.'" In *Revista latinoamericana de teología* 12 (October-December 1995).

Hélder Cámara, Dom. *A Thousand Reasons for Living.* Philadelphia: Fortress Press, 1981.
Hertz, Karl H. *Everyman a Priest.* Philadelphia: Muhlenberg Press, 1960.
Hinkelammert, Franz. "Una sociadad en la que todos quepan. De la impotencia de la omnipotencia." In *PASOS* 60, 1995.
Hollenweger, Walter. *Charismatisch-pfingstliches Christentum.Herkunft, Situation, Oekumenische Chancen.* Göttingen: Vandenhoeck & Ruprecht, 1997.
Kater, John L., Jr.: "Whatever Happened to Liberation Theology?" In *Anglican TheologicalReview* 83 /4 (fall 2001).
Lalive d'Epinay, Christian. *Haven of the Masses: A Study of the Pentecostal Movement in Chile.* Santiago: Editorial del Pacífico, 1969.
---. "Latin American Protestantism in a Revolutionary Context." In *Lutheran Quarterly 22*/1 (February 1970), pp. 29-39.
Laur, Hendrik. "The Skeleton in the Closet: North American Lutherans in Latin America." In *Lutheran Quarterly 22*/1 (February 1970), pp. 40-48.
Lernoux, Penny. *Cry of the People.* Garden City, NY: Doubleday, 1980.
May, Roy H. "La tierra en tiempos de globalización" In *PASOS* 76, 1998.
Míguez Bonino, José. *Christians and Marxists—The Mutual Challenge to Revolution.* Grand Rapids: William Eerdmans, 1976.
---. *Toward a Christian Political Ethics.* Philadelphia: Fortress Press, 1983.
---. "Protestantism's Contribution to Latin America," in *Lutheran Quarterly 22*/1 (February 1970), pp. 92-98.
Miranda, José Porfirio. *Marx and the Bible—A Critique of the Philosophy of Oppression.* Maryknoll, NY: Orbis Books, 1974.
Modrow, Hans . *Die Perestroika.* Berlin: edition ost, 1998.
Nagle, Robin. *Claiming the Virgin—The Broken Promise of Liberation Theology in Brazil.* New York City: Routledge, 1997.
Pixley, George V. (Jorge). "Toward a Latin American Theology: Some Suggestions." In *Lutheran Quarterly* 22/1 (February 1970), pp. 69-78.
Richard, Pablo. "Teología de la solaridad en el contexto actual de Economía neoliberal de libre mercado." In *PASOS* 83 (1999).
Santa Ana, Julio de. *Towards a Church of the Poor.* Maryknoll, NY: Orbis Books, 1979.
---.*El Desafío de los Pobres a la Iglesia.* Costa Rica: Editorial Universitaria "Rodrigo Facio," 1977.
Schuurman, Lambert. "Some Observations on the Relevance of Luther's Theory of the Two Realms for the Theological Task in Latin America." In *Lutheran Quarterly* 22/1 (February 1970), pp. 77-91.
Segundo, Juan Luis. *The Liberation of Theology.* Maryknoll, NY: Orbis Books, 1976.
---. "The Possible Contribution of Protestant Theology to Latin American Christianity in the Future." In *Lutheran Quarterly* 22/1 (February 1970), pp. 60-68.

Shaull, Richard and Cesar, Waldo. *Pentecostalism and the Future of the Christian Churches.* Grand Rapids: William Eerdmans, 2000.

Silva Gotay, Samuel. *El Pensamiento Cristiano Revolucionario en América Latina y el Caribe.* Río Piedra, Puerto Rico: Cordillera/Ediciones Sigueme, 1983.

Sobrino, Jon. *Christology at the Crossroads—A Latin American Approach.* Maryknoll, NY: Orbis Books, 1978.

Stumme, John R. "Luther's Concept of the Two Kingdoms in the Context of Liberation Theology." In *Word and World* 3/4 (Fall 1983), pp. 423-34.

Villapando, Waldo Luis, ed. *Las Iglesias del Trasplante—Protestantismo de Inmigración en la Argentina.* Buenos Aires: Centro de Estudios Cristianos, 1970.

Wingren, Gustaf. *Luther on Vocation.* Philadelphia: Muhlenberg Press, 1957.

Yutzis, Mario."The Revolutionary Process in Latin American Christianity." In *Lutheran Quarterly* 22/1 (February1970), pp. 11-38.

INDEX

Age of Enlightenment and the Protestant Reformation, 85, 95
Althaus, Paul, 21
Altmann, Walter, 56, 69, 83
Alves, Rubem, 2, 29, 40
Andiñach, Pablo, 5, 9, 33, 52-54
Assmann, Hugo, 2, 29, 34, 66-67

Bastian, Jean-Pierre, vi, 56, 60-61, 74, 85
Baum, Gregory, 92-93
Bedford, Nancy, 37, 53-54
Blatezky, Arturo, 29, 57
Boff, Leonardo, 2, 22-25, 30, 70
Bonhoeffer, Dietrich, 30
Brandao Vilela, Avelar, 9
Braun, Rafael, 1, 55
Bultmann, Rudolf, 19-21

Calvin, John, 16, 49
"Centessimus Annus," encyclica, 62-63, 87
Cesar, Waldo, 76-82 passim
Comunidades de base (grass roots communities), 2, 28-29, 41, 48, 52, 56, 77, 95
Croatto, Severino, 2

Detroit Conference, *see* "Theology in the Americas"
Doig, Germán, 48
Donini, Antonio O., vi
Duns Scotus, John, 24
Dussel, Enrique, 2, 26-29, 36, 51, 62, 66-67

Eucharistic Congress, Bogotá, 1968, 6-8, 38, 50
"Evangelii Nuntiandi," encyclica, 37-42, 44, 45, 55, 61
Exodus, 17, 86

Freire Costa, Jurandir, 82
Gallegos, Hector, 27
"Gaudium et spes," Pastoral Constitution, 40, 44
George, William P., 62
Gottwald, Norman, 54
Grass roots communities, *see Comunidades de base*
Gutiérrez, Gustavo, vi, 2, 13-16, 22, 24, 29, 35, 39, 49, 56, 59-60, 65

Hansen, Willy, 13, 52-54
Hélder Câmara, Dom, 7, 11, 28
Herzog, Frederick, 33-34
Hinkelammert, Franz, 67
Hitler, Adolf, 17, 35, 63
Hollenweger, Walter, 74
"Humanae Vitae," encyclica, 7, 12, 61-62, 69

International Monetary Fund, 17, 66, 68
I.S.E.D.E.T. (Instituto Superior Evangélico de Estudios Teológicos), panel discussion, vi, 2, 51-55, 70, 90
Itatí (Buenos Aires ghetto), 57

"Jesus Dominus," declaration, 16
John XXIII, Pope, 5, 7, 50
John Paul II, Pope, 43, 62

Käsemann, Elisabeth, 36
Kater, John L, Jr., 65-72 passim
Kissinger, Henry, 65
Kuss, Otto, 21

Lalive d'Epinay, Christian, 60, 73-76, 80
Lortz, Joseph, 26
Luther, Martin, 7, 14-15, 16, 23, 30, 40, 49, 63, 83-95

Marxism, 2, 5, 11, 21-22, 28, 30, 35, 45, 51, 53-54, 63, 66, 68, 72, 82, 90-91, 92-93
"Mater et Magistra," encyclica, 87
May, Roy H., 70
Medellín Conference of Latin American Bishops (CELAM), 1968, 2, 6, 9-12, 13, 15, 48-49, 51, 55, 60, 70, 74
Méndez Arceo, Sergio, 28
Michel, Otto, 21
Míguez Bonino, José, 2, 29, 53-54
Militarism, vi, 2, 11, 34-36, 41, 50, 51, 63, 80-81
Miranda, José Porfirio, 2, 20-22, 24, 30
Moltmann, Juergen, 40
Movement for Basic Education, Brazil, 28

Nagle, Robin, v-vi

"Pacem in Terris," encyclica, 87
Paul VI, Pope, vi, 6-8, 11-12, 37-42, 43, 44
Pentacostalism, 60, 73-82
Pereira Neto, Henrique, 27
Piedra, Arturo, 68
Pietrantonio, Ricardo, 19, 51, 52-54 passim
Pironio, Eduardo, 9
Pixley, George (Jorge), 93
"Populorum Progressio," encyclica, 11, 87
Preferential option for the poor, 43-50, 85, 93
Puebla Conference of Latin American Bishops (CELAM), 1979, vi, 43-50, 55, 61, 72, 93 See also Preferential option for the poor

"Quadrogesimo Anno," encyclica, 89
Quilmes (Buenos Aires suburb), 73

"Rerum Novarum," encyclica, 87
Richard, Pablo, 66, 71
Romero, Oscar, 57

Santa Ana, Julio de, 2, 29
Schuurman, Lambert, 89, 94

Second Vatican Council, 5, 12, 15, 40

Segundo, Juan Luis, 1, 2, 5, 9, 19-20, 23, 40-41, 50, 59, 94
Shaull, Richard and Cesar, Waldo, study of Brazilian Pentecostals, 76-82
Sobrino, Jon, 2, 25-26, 30

"Theology in the Americas," Detroit conference, 1975, 33-34, 54, 70
Torres, Camilo, 27-28
Tutu, Desmond, 61

Valdivieso, Antonio de, 27
von Rad, Gerhard, 21

Weber, Max, 63
Wesley, Charles and John, 16

Zimmerli, Walter, 21
Zwingli, Ulrich, 49

AUTHOR BIOGRAPHICAL SKETCH

A native of Dresden, Germany, Manfred Kurt Bahmann studied theology at the universities of Göttingen, Heidelberg and Bonn. After an exchange year at the United Theological Seminary in Dayton, Ohio he received the American M.Div. degree in 1954 and the following year was ordained into the German Church of the Palatinate. He completed the first and second German theological examinations in 1956 and 1958 while serving as a Labor Service chaplain on NATO bases in West Germany.

In 1959 Bahmann came to the United States with his American wife Marianne, a musician. After serving a Lutheran parish in West Virginia he completed Ph.D. studies in Reformation history at the Hartford Seminary Foundation. In 1965 he was sent by the LCA Board of Missions to Argentina as Professor for Church History at the Facultad Luterana de Teología in José C. Paz and the United Theological Seminary (I.S.E.D.E.T.) in Buenos Aires. He returned to the United States with his family in 1970.

A rostered pastor of the Evangelical Lutheran Church in America (ELCA) for forty-five years, the author has been campus pastor at Stanford University and New York University; held pastorates in California, West Virginia, New York City and West Berlin; and presently serves a Lutheran congregation in eastern Pennsylvania. He has authored many articles and lectured widely on church history and Latin American Liberation Theology.

A Preference for the Poor was published in German under the title *Der Vorzug der Armen*.